FROM WITCH DOCTOR TO BIOFEEDBACK
The Story of Healing by Suggestion

Anxiety about disease has been a primary human concern since the beginning of civilization. Before people knew anything about the functioning of the human body, sickness was attributed to hostile forces working either from within or outside the body. Those powers had to be driven out, chased away, or pacified by ceremonies which strongly impressed the minds of the sick. Through the power of suggestion, temporary cures were often effected, especially when the symptoms were caused by emotional conditions. Such acts of healing, real or imaginary, have continued to this day, side by side with the advance of scientific medicine. From Witch Doctor to Biofeedback *is a journey through a fascinating subject filled with such exotic fare as witch doctors and medicine men, voodoo and exorcism, faith healers and Christian Scientists, mesmerism and hypnotism.*

BOOKS BY ALFRED APSLER

COMMUNES THROUGH THE AGES
The Search for Utopia

FIGHTER FOR INDEPENDENCE
Jawaharlal Nehru

FROM WITCH DOCTOR TO BIOFEEDBACK
The Story of Healing by Suggestion

IVAN THE TERRIBLE

PROPHET OF REVOLUTION
Karl Marx

THE SUN KING
Louis XIV of France

"VIVE DE GAULLE"
The Story of Charles de Gaulle

FROM WITCH DOCTOR TO BIOFEEDBACK

The Story of Healing by Suggestion

ALFRED APSLER

JULIAN MESSNER ⬤ NEW YORK

Copyright © 1977 by Alfred Apsler
Second Printing, 1978
Printed in the United States of America

Design by Irving Perkins

Library of Congress Cataloging in Publication Data

Apsler, Alfred.
  From witch doctor to biofeedback.

  Bibliography: p. 185
  Includes index.
  SUMMARY: Discusses various methods of healing through
the ages that rely on the power of suggestion including witch
doctors, medicine men, voodoo, exorcism, faith healing, Christian
Science, mesmerism, and hypnosis.
  1. Mental healing—History—Juvenile literature. 2. Thera-
peutics, Suggestive—History—Juvenile literature. [1. Mental
healing—History. 2. Parapsychology] I. Title.
RZ400.A83   615'.851'09   76-56425
ISBN 0-671-32832-8 lib. bdg.

Hc5/14

TO ERNA AND RUBY
IN APPRECIATION AND LOVE

A physician is successful when the patient believes in him.

GIROLAMO CARDANO

Of all the bodies in nature, none is so potent in its influence upon man as is the body of man himself.

FRANZ ANTON MESMER

Day by day, in every way, I am getting better and better.

EMIL COUÉ

Contents

CHAPTER ONE

Shamans Make Housecalls

THE WOMEN and children huddled close together on the narrow platforms at the entrance to the huts, coarse dwellings of wood and bark which hung from wooden poles sunk into the lakebed. The lodges swayed back and forth three feet above the dark-green water. Gusty winds rippled the mountain lake, and from afar the glaciers gleamed in all their grandeur. This setting was a tiny cluster of pole huts fashioned by a Stone Age people who lived some eight thousand years ago in what is today Switzerland.

In the early morning the men had gone out on their rafts made of rough timbers bound together by strips of bark. In order to feed themselves and their families, the men fished in the lake and hunted along the shore.

Now the sun was only a crimson glow barely seen on the horizon. Soon it would be dark. The men should have been back long ago. The old, the very young, and the women shivered in the cold wind that came from the high mountain peaks. They wrapped their loose clothing made of hide and plant fiber matting tighter around their bodies. They were waiting for the bringers of nourishment. Without them, there would be hunger tonight and starvation tomorrow. Soon they would be faced with the extinction that had been the lot of so many other clans. The men had often told stories about them. One of the younger women suddenly let out a shrill yell. She spoke no words, but everyone instantly knew the meaning of the shout: the men were coming. Movement immediately replaced the tense stillness of the group. Shouts of relief rang out. The continued life was assured, at least for a few more days.

But as the rafts moved closer to the shore, it became apparent that something was wrong. The men paddled in silence, their backs arched strongly and their faces hidden. There was none of the usual chanting announcing the success of the expedition and the approach of food. On the platforms of the pole houses faces fell in dejection, eyes strained, and mouths gaped in fear of the bad news.

Bad luck had indeed visited the fishermen, but it could have been worse. Nobody had been killed by a mother bear worried about her cubs. Nobody had fallen from a cliff or into a crevice in the forbidding alpine wilderness. The men had even brought back a load of trout. They threw the fish on the banked embers of the cooking fire. There were also some rabbits and a sizable pile of wild grain from the muddy lake bank, enough for both an evening meal and leftovers to be eaten for the next several days.

Suddenly one woman broke into a drawn-out wail of despair, and her four children immediately joined in, as they watched a man supported by the sturdy arms of two companions being dragged from the lead raft. They placed him gingerly on a pile of hides inside the largest hut.

"Mauck, are you alive?" wailed his wife.

A tortured groan escaped the man's pale lips. The color had drained from the weather-creased cheeks of the man who was the band's acknowledged chief. Cold perspiration had matted his long hair and the dark brown whiskers. He seemed to fight for breath, and the odor of vomit enveloped his body.

The hunters answered the unasked questions of the distraught woman.

"He has no wounds. Nobody attacked him. But suddenly, he collapsed. He winced and his body jerked around in terrible contortions. He screamed and screamed. He had just eaten some bright red berries from a bush. We had never tasted that kind of berry and we were afraid to try. But you know Mauck. He has no fear of anything."

The woman wrung her hands, then tore at her long hair as if she wanted to pull it from her scalp. "An evil spirit has entered his body, the spirit of the red berry. He was the bravest hunter and warrior. If he dies we will all perish in the long winter months. Aiiiiiii!" Her cries of mourning and fear echoed from the mountain wall across the lake.

Mauck lay motionless on the layer of hides. His body was exhausted by the cruel torments of vomiting and diarrhea. His breathing was so shallow that it seemed as if it might stop at any moment. The woman and the four children squatted around the prostrate body numb with fear.

A tall figure entered the hut, bending low to clear the crossbeam. The person did not look like the other members of the clan. On first impression, he was both terrifying and soothing at the same time. A mask fashioned from a bear's snout hid his face. The skins of several small animals were wrapped around the gaunt body, but they could not completely conceal the deformed shoulders and sunken chest. A long furry tail was fastened to the figure's lower back. The individual was a priest who used magic to cure the sick, to divine the hidden, and to control events. This strange human being, the shaman, bent over the stricken man, shaking his head.

Mauck's eyes opened to a narrow slit. He dimly made out the shape of the shaman who had begun to dance in great hops and jumps around the bed of hides. Without interrupting his movements, the shaman began to chant, switching from a high piping voice to a deep bass. Muffled by the bear's mask, the voice sounded eerie. It made sounds beyond anything human vocal chords usually produce. The chanting was accompanied by the rhythmic rattle of many small bones, shells, and pebbles that were draped in chains around the man's neck, waist, and ankles. The tuneless noises gradually lulled the witnesses into a hypnotic half-sleep. Slowly, their bodies began to sway forward and backward.

A scream pierced the monotony. The oldest child jumped to his feet in terror. "The hut is shaking!" he shouted. Perhaps a storm was coming up over the lake. But inside the crowded lodge nobody doubted that it was the shaman's magic that made the dwelling shiver and the beams creak.

From the wide folds of his robe, the healer drew out a puppet of straw and rags. His chant grew to a wild roar as he hurled the puppet into the fire. One moment the flames had burned feebly, the next they flared up high as if driven by some unseen power.

The shaman's movements became more frenzied. With his long arms he seemed to stab at an unseen enemy. It was a ferocious struggle, but only one of the opponents was visible. The healer's bony fingers gripped a wooden wand which he swung like a weapon to drive away the death-breathing foe.

At one point in the battle, he seemed to weaken. Like his patient on the floor, he appeared to be close to death. But then he staged his own revival, obviously setting an example for the stricken warrior to follow.

He demanded that the woman cut slivers from three of Mauck's fingernails. He mixed them in a bowl with some strange powder which he had brought with him, and chanted over the mixture. Then, swinging the bowl over his head, he threw the contents into the fire. As he turned away from the flames, he was gripped by convulsions. His limbs thrashed about, forming distorted angles in the dark shadows.

Hour after hour the shaman kept up his performance. It was late at night when he finally broke down in complete exhaustion. The mask dropped to reveal a face that was deathly pale except for blobs of paint that were now beginning to streak down the cheeks. Sweat and paint had combined in a sticky mess.

It seemed that the healer had taken on the symptoms of his patient's illness, while, in the meantime, Mauck's breathing had become stronger and more regular. When the morning sun blinked through the chinks of grass and mud that formed the roof, the patient was sleeping soundly. The shaman rose from the floor, painfully rubbing his aching joints. Hoarse from the long abuse of his vocal chords, he gave instructions to the woman who had not moved from her place all night.

"I will grind the tip of a deer's horn into the juice of the herbs found on the island out there and you make him drink it. Then fry him a dish of a mouse and a toad. And be sure to make him wear this from now on." He handed her a shriveled little leather bag, dirty with much handling. From the noise it produced, it seemed to contain several pebbles or pieces of bone. The next step in the treatment was a rubdown of the sleeping man with a strong-smelling liquid which the healer had brought with him in a small clay bottle.

A picture of utter weariness, the shaman finally turned to go. Then he stopped. He had just remembered a most important measure. "Tell him he must go back to the place where he fell sick. He must go before the next full moon and leave a gift there for the spirit of the berry so the spirit will not return and make him sick again. If he wants to live long he must make sure to do this."

Then he was gone. The chief remained in a semicoma for

another two days. He slowly recovered, and the first time that he was able to leave his own hut, he took presents to the hut of the shaman—a beautiful flint knife he had fashioned shortly before the mishap, a hood of deerskin, and some fish.

Who was this man who put on the dramatic performance? A doctor? Certainly not, at least not in the modern sense. He knew nothing about blood circulation or the functions of the heart and lungs, and even less about infection and the causes of disease. Through experience and handed-down knowledge, he had learned about many plants that had a healing effect and foods or liquids that gave strength. He could bind up wounds so that the injured would not bleed to death. He also understood that complete rest helped to restore health. Beyond that, he was as ignorant as the patient. He had just experienced many different situations and had taken the time to reflect upon them.

Had Mauck died from the poison, his fate would have come as no great surprise. Death was the constant companion of early people. They were surrounded by hostile forces, which confronted them in the guise of foul weather, ferocious animals, and other humans who competed with them for the sparse resources of food and shelter. Life was but a short interval between birth and death.

If the shaman had lost his patient, the disappointed survivors might have turned against him. They might have killed him or driven him from the compound to face the hostile forest wilderness in solitude. These were the risks of the occupation.

A wise shaman could avoid such trouble for himself, however, by asserting that he would certainly have been successful had the patient followed his directions properly. Or perhaps the stricken person had violated some dangerous taboo. Even so, the shaman's reputation would have been severely damaged. Such a mishap could have given a rival shaman just the chance he had been waiting for. He could now come forward and take over the dominant role of healer for the band. But more often than not, the reigning shaman could weather such crises because people were afraid of his magic powers. They believed that he was able not only to cure them, but also to make them ill and worse. His secret connections with the spirit world could be used for evil as well as for good.

Mauck recovered. Was it because of the magic ministrations of the healer, or because Mauck's body was hardened by the rugged outdoor life, by constant physical exertion, and by a sparse but healthy diet? Whatever it was, the shaman received the credit. The respect given him by the band was complete. He was the real power in the life of the little group. Even the chief did not dare to embark on any important action without first obtaining the shaman's advice. The shaman was a healer, but also a counselor, minister, and general problem solver.

To find a shaman one did not have to hike to a remote Swiss lake. He could be found on all continents, wherever human beings had joined together to form some sort of a rudimentary society. We have many names for the person who filled the shaman's functions: medicine man, witch doctor, sorcerer, priest.

The profession of healing can truly be called the world's oldest. The shamans and their various counterparts were the first members of a human community who became specialists, who did (or at least were thought to be able to do) what the others could not do. All the rest of the tribe practiced the same trade, providing the wherewithall for staying alive. This arrangement prevailed wherever the human species could be found, from the arctic to the tropics, in the eastern and western hemispheres.

When an Algonquin warrior was wounded by a raiding band of another tribe of Indians, the medicine man showed up in a grotesque outfit sewn together from the skins of deformed large animals. The creatures of nature were believed to have special powers. From the medicine man's costume dangled dried snakes, the withered bodies of small birds, and the hoofs of slain deer. With his piercing yells, the medicine man tried to imitate animal voices. In his hand he held a rattle that he shook in accompaniment to his shouting and singing.

From time to time he stopped his wild jumps long enough to throw herbs and dried tobacco leaves on the fire. Soon the air was filled with a pungent smoke. At long last, the healer bent over the stricken warrior and carefully extracted the arrow from his side. A sticky ointment was applied, not to the patient, but to the offending weapon, which was treated as if it were a living being. The medicine man talked to it, repeating the same string of words over and over.

Then the Indian healer put his mouth over the wound in order to suck out the evil that had entered through the opening. He called for water, and after washing the patient, he massaged him with strong fingers.

Finally, seeing that the wounded man, though weak from the loss of blood, showed signs of consciousness, the medicine man crouched low over the mat on the floor, almost touching the brave's ear with his lips. He began to question him.

"Did you go hunting on a day when it was forbidden?" "Did you set foot in the sacred grove where only I am allowed to enter?" "Did you forget to chant the life-preserving chant as the battle began?"

The medicine man was concerned with what taboo the ailing man had violated, and what sacred rules he had broken that caused the mishap.

Should the patient die, should the poison of the arrow and the loss of blood be too much for the mistreated body, the medicine man would know the reason: it was the revenge of the spirits for the violation of the rules which he had taught his people. The spirits were so angry that even he who knew their likes and dislikes could not soothe their feelings. With illness and death, they inflicted punishment on man.

Had the Algonquin warrior died of his wound, it would have been a severe loss to the whole tribe. Each person's contribution to the small band was vital. The strain on the whole community would have been even greater had he lingered on as a weakened invalid. Not only would he not have been able to carry his share in the fierce battle for survival, but others would have had to care for him. Time and strength which were desperately needed for the common struggle would have been lost.

Not only the sick and the wounded, but also their families and the entire band to which they belonged put all their hopes in the wisdom and skill of the medicine man. His was a grave responsibility.

~~~~~~

CHAPTER TWO

Witch and Other Doctors

PRIMITIVE PEOPLE were surrounded by forces they did not understand. Nor were they able to combat these forces. Their bodies suffered wounds from attacks and from accidents in the forest and desert and on the waters. Food poisoning, rheumatism, arthritis, tooth decay, and diseases caused by heat and frost, by floods and draughts, by famine and infection, led to excruciating pain. No method was known by which the roots of all these many forms of suffering could be laid bare. Still, humans never ceased to search for explanations and, armed with the explanations, for weapons to combat pain.

And then there was death. In those days, it came at an early age for most men and women. Primitive people pondered the nature of death. What did it mean? What happened to the parent, the child, the husband, or wife who no longer moved or spoke, and soon turned into a foul, loathsome object? Were the dead dangerous to the living? What was one to do to prevent the departed from causing harm?

These questions defied satisfactory answers. For many members of the human race they still do. In their frightened insecurity, early beings turned to the shaman and the medicine man, not only for answers, but also for action to avert real and imagined dangers.

Men and women were taught by the healer-teacher-priest that pain and death were caused by beings similar to themselves, but ones who were invisible and immensely more powerful. Such creatures resided in forests and meadows, inside mountains and under the surface of rivers, in the skies and in the bodies of animals.

The Stone Age tribesman knew how to defend himself against a human enemy, even against a bear, wolf, or mountain lion, provided that the group worked together as a team. But how would a food-gatherer influence those invisible forces, those spirits dwelling beyond his reach?

A spirit could enter a human body at will. Every misfortune was attributed to spirits. They were particularly blamed for causing insanity.

Once evil spirits had taken possession of someone, how could they be ejected? The members of the tribe did not know. Therefore, they responded with great relief and gratitude when one of their own tribe came forward and maintained that he did know. This extraordinary person could communicate with the hidden powers, could even humor them so that they would do no harm to the tribe. Perhaps he could even get the spirits to favor the group with health and bounty. Wasn't it worth it to shower that individual with gifts, to make him a powerful leader, even at times the master of life and death? Sometimes the shaman was a woman, and the same reverence was given to her.

The witch doctor claimed that he knew how to contact the departed ancestors. If he treated them as they desired, they would leave the living alone or even come to their assistance. Ancestor worship was an important aspect of the quest for security and was, at one time, practiced in many parts of the world.

The shaman knew or pretended to know which chants, dances, costumes, charms, and amulets, and which scents, gestures, and rituals would be favorably received by the spirits or ghosts. If he felt that efforts to please them were hopeless, he tried to frighten them away by making horrible noises. It was also believed that some spirits feared water and others smoke, and still others took off in a hurry when certain magic words were spoken.

Let us assume that you don't believe in the existence of demons which invade people's lives, of ghosts that drop boulders on unsuspecting hunters, of spirits that cause madness and convulsions. How then would you explain the fact that witch doctors and other healers like them could boast of an impressive number of successes? We will see in the pages of this volume that untold millions of people have preserved their trust in similar healers all through the ages, up to and including our own time.

It is not hard to see that those practitioners with their magic wands and their unsavory brews were bound to pick up, through trial and error, if nothing else, many pieces of practical knowledge. They were on safe ground when they dispensed wholesome herbs, when they bled wounds to remove the venom of snakes, when they counseled rest and cleanliness. The bark of some trees and the glands of certain animals acted as laxatives or induced vomiting, thereby diluting poisons in the body. Other potions relieved rheumatism and dropsy.

A few of the herbs used by prehistoric healers are still in use in modern pharmacies. Excavations have shown that occasionally a Stone Age doctor even performed brain surgery, and the results were not always fatal.

But all these skills do not fully explain the reasons for the prescientific healer's success. We know today that 50 to 80 percent of the clients sitting in a doctor's waiting room suffer from *psychosomatic* illnesses. Their chills and headaches, their diarrhea, and even the paralysis of their arms or legs are real and cause pain. But the physician can discover nothing abnormal in the body that can account for the trouble. The cause is a mental or emotional problem, such as fear, insecurity, frustration, or lack of love and attention. Pills, ointments, and even operations will reduce the discomfort for a time, but will not get at the root of the disturbance.

The lake dweller and the early Indian had their psychosomatic problems, also. And the shaman's performances were as good a countermeasure as any.

The people in those times also came down with many of the same illnesses that plague us today. We know now that the human body possesses an astounding amount of resilience. A goodly number of sick people would eventually get well with or without medical help. Our built-in recuperative powers are strong, and they were probably stronger in earlier periods.

But while the pain and the fear of deathly illness lasted, the rites of the medicine man were of great help simply because the patient believed them to be helpful. Pain can be soothed, at least for a time, by distracting the mind. The medicine man found this out through direct insight and long experience. The dancing and the singing of the shaman distracted the patient's attention from the pain. When a baby cries because of a scraped knee, the mother dangles a toy and the father makes funny faces. Soon the baby has forgotten the injured knee.

This distraction can be particularly quick and strong when the healing ceremony is charged with high emotion. It is an unusual experience, just as an unexpected visit by a close friend, the winning of a much coveted prize, or a very impressive artistic performance might be for a modern person. Under such an emotional impact, we are suddenly aware that the nagging headache has disappeared or that the upset stomach seems to have quieted down.

The primitive healer was also in the manufacturing business. He made charms from bones, feathers, metal, and wood. His clients were supposed to wear them around their necks or ankles, hang them over the hearth, or fasten them to the gable of the lodge. In this way, they would protect the home from fire, ward off hostile spears and knives, keep the lover from straying, and, of course, prevent illness. If everything went all right, the charm or amulet received the credit.

Primitive, you say? What about the rabbit's foot inside the modern car—or the plastic figures on the dashboard? It is true that they are not pagan idols, but the figures of Christian saints. Yet the purpose of placing them in the car is similar to that of nailing a horseshoe on the doorpost of an old house.

The shaman's performance had to be dramatic, entertaining, and awe-inspiring. It was hard, skillful work that required long training. The practitioner often worked himself into a state of complete exhaustion. The danger of him becoming ill or even dying was real. At times, the healing session took on the character of a duel between healer and evil spirit. The onlookers—and probably the healer himself—strongly believed that the angered demon was not beyond hurting or destroying the shaman in such a combat. As an act of revenge, the demon might also leave the body of the patient and enter that of the healer.

No wonder that a person who would take such terrible risks in the service of his neighbors gained a special place of esteem in their hearts. The simple food-gatherers and herders turned to him not only for relief from pain, but also for guidance in other trying situations. Could he make a childless woman conceive, and so prevent her from becoming an outcast?

If a tribesman's cattle became sick, obviously a malevolent neighbor had cast an evil spell on the animals. Could the wise man counteract the magic spell by an even stronger counter-magic?

In such a society, everybody was thought capable of manipulating the unseen forces, either intentionally or by accident. The average man or woman could cast spells and perform magic rituals. But the witch doctor, who was a specialist, knew his craft better than all the part-time sorcerers. His own special magic should easily outperform the magic of anybody else, unless his competitor was an even more accomplished witch doctor.

The healer was sought out to give advice for all sorts of personal concerns, and the more he became acquainted with the problems of his flock, the greater practical wisdom he acquired.

As the obvious middleman between mere humans and the powers beyond, he went into action when the existence of the community was threatened by too much or too little rain. He knew what gifts would please the spirits, what sort of dancing and chanting would entertain them so that they would grant plentiful catches to the fisherman and victory to the warrior.

Such functions gave the healer the position of religious leader or priest also. He not only passed on the requests of the people to the immortals, he also explained what those spirits were like. He wove tales about their deeds and habits, and from that he proceeded to speculate on the origin of humans and on their role and duties in the limited world that they knew. As the earliest teacher of philosophy and theology in a society that knew no books and no schools, he satisfied the curiosity of human beings and found for them a place in the puzzling universe.

The healer also assumed the task of laying down rules of behavior. What were the duties of the male, the female, the head of the family, the warrior? What places were taboo and at what times? What actions and what words had to be avoided so as not to arouse the anger of the spirit world?

How did a man or a woman become a shaman? In quite a few communities, the position was hereditary. The child of the healer grew up knowing that he would follow the father's occupation. This trend of keeping jobs of all kinds within the family is a very old one, and in many parts of the world it continued until recent times.

The training for the job was a kind of apprenticeship. By many years of informal contact, the shaman-to-be learned his trade. He lived in the house of the master and accompanied him on his errands. He had to swear not to pass on to outsiders what was revealed to him by the master. While modern scientists publish their findings in books and journals, the old shaman surrounded himself with an air of secrecy. His actions had to remain a mystery to his followers. In this way, nobody could challenge his position.

The medicine man was expected to dress and behave differently from ordinary people. Hides of rare or deformed animals, parts of little creatures or whole mummified bodies, feathers, stones, curiously shaped objects of wood, bone, or flint, painted masks and headdresses—all this contributed to the awe which his performance was designed to arouse. For this purpose, he used a wide variety of props, including things to see, sounds to hear, and scents to smell. All the stage effects contributed to the impression that the shaman could do what others could not.

The mystery surrounding the healer was heightened by periodic disappearances. He would stay in his own hut or go out into the dreaded wilderness for prolonged periods. Since a precarious sort of security existed only within the camp and in the company of a number of tribesmen, any such solo forays into forest, desert, or jungle were extremely dangerous.

The excursions meant exposing oneself to hunger, thirst, intense heat or cold, sleeplessness, and the attacks of wild creatures. These wanderings were tremendous acts of personal courage.

The periods of solitude were also part of the training. They gave the candidate opportunity for concentrated undisturbed thought. This might lead to prolonged periods of trance. In a trance a person is half-conscious, as if suspended midway between the states of sleeping and waking. He feels removed from his accustomed surroundings, although he remains in the same place. His mind is focused on one single concern and emptied of all competing thoughts. In a trance one is believed to have deeper insights, a "heightened state of consciousness," as modern mystics put it. People in a trance can do things beyond their normal capacities and obey impulses which they would otherwise resist. We will encounter this phenomenon again in the discussion of psychic healing, hypnotism, and certain forms of religious healing.

An experienced shaman could train himself to go into a trance, not only when alone in the wilderness, but even at the bedside of a patient surrounded by his wailing family. He would squat, his body completely relaxed, eyes closed, facial muscles strangely altered. The sounds he uttered belonged to no language known by anybody present. He might address invisible beings. All influences from the surrounding world were shut out. The shaman in a trance would not react to questions, to touch, even to the sting of a needle or the heat of burning embers.

In all likelihood, many a witch doctor was himself mentally deranged. But this only increased the high regard of his fellow tribesmen. Whether he reported what was revealed to him while he was in a trance, or whether his disjointed mind just produced an incomprehensible babbling, the assembled followers listened with wonder and amazement.

Much of the medicine man's success rested on the power of suggestion. In the art of domination over other people, suggestion is a most effective tool. It has been used consistently by parents, teachers, politicians, religious leaders, and, not sparingly, by healers whether they sported medical diplomas or not. Strong, vivid suggestion makes the receiver firmly believe in the power of the suggester and also in his own capacity to succeed.

In the world of the shaman, illness was brought about by invisible spirits. Disease was a form of punishment for the breaking of taboos. Such views prevailed unchallenged for thousands of years. Only comparatively late in the course of human history did the thought arise that illness was a natural consequence of natural disturbances in the human body; that ghosts, spells, and black magic had nothing to do with it. Hippocrates, who lived in Greece in the fifth and fourth centuries B.C., was the first to point this out in clear and forceful language. He is regarded as the father of medicine as we know it today: an applied natural science.

It was an irony of fate that the same Hippocrates who had banished the gods from the sickroom was made into a god himself after his death. He definitely would not have liked the idea, but it was the greatest honor that his admirers knew to bestow upon him. Greek and Roman doctors were known to keep his statue on a pedestal in their consulting chambers. When they had to examine a patient suffering from a baffling ailment, they turned to the likeness of the great healer, hoping that, in his now divine state, he would furnish them with an instant diagnosis of the disease.

But for many centuries after the flowering of ancient Greek civilization, the voice of Hippocrates was lost in an outgrowth of general ignorance. People continued to look at almost everything except the machinery of the human body to find out the cause of disease. It was not until the sixteenth century A.D. that scholars began to seriously question ideas that had been accepted since prehistoric times.

The struggle between the old and new viewpoints was difficult, and sometimes violent. The dispensers of charms and magic did not give up easily. A man who stood in the midst of this struggle and could fight on both sides was Paracelsus. Paracelsus, like so many other men ahead of their times, was beset by inner conflicts and by hostile critics and competitors. Much of his adult life was spent running from persecution. He finally died in poverty in 1541.

Paracelsus made his living as a healer, and in order to get patients, he had to do what other healers of the time did. Therefore, he made his diagnoses by the stars. He checked whether the patient's problem was caused by the spell of an evil sorcerer, and he dispensed charms and miracle-working stones.

But when the same Paracelsus became a professor of medicine at the University of Basel, he ridiculed the idea that ghosts had anything to do with illness. His unorthodox lectures outraged his learned colleagues so much that they drove him from his post.

In the manner of many medieval scholars, Paracelsus combined healing with alchemy. He spent many long hours in laboratories trying to make gold from various chemicals. He never succeeded—nor did any of the others. But while engaged in his obscure experiments, Paracelsus hit upon the idea that certain combinations of elements naturally affect the chemistry of the human body. Here were the real remedies for aches and disorders. Paracelsus pioneered the science of pharmacology. When the doctor today routinely writes out a prescription and the druggist fills it promptly, they are continuing what was begun by Paracelsus, the Renaissance doctor.

Since the years of his discoveries, we have collected vast

amounts of insight into the functions of our bodies. Many once-fatal diseases have become harmless. Our physicians heal with the help of chemicals and diets, through operations, casts, massages, and many other forms of therapy.

But even though an almost unbelievable arsenal of scientific weapons has been fashioned to fight disease, there are still crippling disorders which have not yet been conquered. Frightening breakdowns of the human mind still occur without the possibility of correction. Nothing much can be done to stem the inexorable onward course of aging, and death still looms at the end of the road.

This explains why the shaman is still with us, not only in remote, supposedly uncivilized regions, but also in our modern cities and rural villages. He may call himself by different names, but his basic approach is still the same. He still exercises his capacity for suggestion and tries to instill trust and confidence in the patient. He manipulates emotions and creates an environment that will make the client ready to register strong impressions.

Even the modern scientific healer with the imposing medical degree is not above using some of the age-old techniques of the witch doctor to supplement the tools of office, laboratory, and clinic now at his disposal.

Unlike the shaman of old, the physician of the twentieth century sticks to the art of healing and leaves religious functions and the enforcement of moral codes to others. He does not, as a rule, control the leaders of government anymore, nor does he routinely give advice to the lovelorn or locate missing treasures. Yet the general prestige of the medical profession is still very high. Many people today still approach the doctor as if he could work miracles. With infinite respect, they listen to what he has to say even when he passes judgment on matters which have little or nothing to do with medicine.

~~~~~~

CHAPTER THREE

The Medicine Man Still Makes Rounds

THE CAVE PEOPLE are gone. So are the Swiss lake dwellers and their pole huts. But the medicine man still makes the rounds of sickbeds in places where modern science has not yet arrived. On some South Pacific islands, in remote areas of tropical Africa, and in the most inaccessible reaches of the Brazilian jungle, people continue to 'exist in a Stone Age culture. They have never heard of x-rays, injections, or blood transfusions.

An Indian woman who has just given birth to a baby boy cringes in pain. She lies almost doubled up on a thin mat which is all that separates her wasted body from the dirt floor. The small band to which she belongs lives on a remote tributary of the Amazon River that is still almost untouched by modern civilization.

The medicine man, dressed in strips of brightly colored cloth and wearing a headdress of bird feathers, approaches the mat. He calmly observes the whimpering girl, who is still practically a child herself. He takes his time while the young mother's relatives shrink away in fear, ready to disappear into the green thicket of the jungle.

Having assessed the situation, the healer produces a pipe from under his clothes, fills it with greenish tobacco leaves, and begins to inhale. At the same time, he shakes a rattle which produces an unnerving squeak. He swallows the blue tobacco smoke in deep gulps until he passes out or pretends to. While he lies there prone on the hard ground apparently overcome by smoke inhalation, the spirits are supposed to tell him what he needs to know.

After a long time he rises, seemingly recovered, and turns to the shivering and perspiring girl. Now he blows curls of tobacco smoke in the direction of her abdomen. He alternates the smoke-blowing with massaging. In this way, he intends to drive out whatever does not belong in there. Something must have gotten into the body by magic forces. Now an even more powerful magic effort is needed to bring it out again.

The medicine man lets out a triumphant shout as he holds aloft a small piece of animal bone. "Look here, all you good people!" he shouts. "This is what the evil sorcerer has caused to enter the girl's stomach. Now she will be all right." Accompanied by murmurs of praise and clutching several gratefully proffered gifts, he departs without revealing that he had shrewdly palmed the object before he started the "operation."

Do we call this deception? It is obvious that this is what it was since the medicine man came well prepared for his juggling trick. But it must be admitted that he not only added to his own prestige, but was also of definite help to the patient. Looking at the little piece of bone in the healer's hand, the young woman felt her pain and anxiety recede. A wonderful feeling of relief surged not only through her mind, but also through the minds of her parents and her brothers and sisters.

This scene was not enacted thousands of years ago. It happened just recently. We know all the details because it was observed by a pair of American anthropologists who had won the trust and friendship of the tribe.

They found the medicine man to be a part-time professional. Along with the other members of the tribe, he searches for food in the jungle and in the river, or he tinkers with his rattles and feathers. All the implements needed for the healing performance are handmade. When the need arises, he slips easily from the food-gathering chores into the role of respected and feared healer.

Whether the medicine man finds his client ill or injured or stark raving mad, he attributes all troubles to the same set of causes. A tree that has crushed a hunter's leg was prompted by supernatural forces to fall on him, and so was the lightning that caused another's hut to burn to the ground. In both cases, black magic is likely to be involved. The medicine man's task is to find out who put the hex on the victim and to render it harmless by his own black magic.

The lot of the medicine man is not an easy one. The danger of assassination is always present. When some misfortune befalls a neighbor, the victim might blame it on the local shaman, or rather on the shaman's power to unleash mischief-making evil spirits. But more often than not, this very belief in the man's special powers keeps even those who dislike him at arm's length.

Most of our religions teach us that every person has a soul, but they do not connect the soul with illness of the body. Primitive people do, especially when confronted by emotional illness. A sixty-three-year-old Guatemalan Indian woman became very agitated. She showed all the signs of what we would call extreme depression. The witch doctor was called in, and after observing the woman for a while, he gave the verdict that she had lost her soul. The soul had somehow left the body and was floating around out there in space. It was his task to get the soul to return to its proper place. If he succeeded, the woman would be cured.

The healing process began with strict questioning. Illness is thought of as a punishment. The patient confessed that there had been bad feelings between her and her husband and it was her fault. She had failed to be a proper wife. After the questioning was finished, the actual healing ceremony began, and continued from early afternoon until about five in the morning. It was anything but a private session. On the contrary, the healer insisted that a number of witnesses had to be present to hear him plead with the spirits for the return of the woman's soul. When he finally left, the woman was physically ill with exhaustion, but she was calm and seemed happier. And, at least according to the healer, she was again in possession of her soul.

The old medicine man does not survive only in the trackless jungle. Even where automobile and airplane, guns and soft drinks have made their appearance, the descendent of the prehistoric healer still plies his trade, sometimes only a short distance away from modern clinics and hospitals with wellstocked pharmacies and intensive-care units. He may even wear modern clothing and pick up some pointers from his white-coated competitors.

Eduardo lives in a Peruvian village. To support his wife and nine children, he used to work as a stevedore. Later he acquired the skills needed to restore Incan artifacts, especially the brilliant friezes which the archaeologists had unearthed. Eduardo has had no formal schooling, but he reads books on philosophy, psychology, and modern hygiene, and he devoutly carries out the practices of the Catholic religion. He is a good restorer, but everybody in the poverty-stricken villages of the area knows that Eduardo is mainly a *curandero*, a folk healer.

Eduardo does not take money for his services. He does not expect a fee, but the poor folks leave small gifts anyway.

What Eduardo practices is a curious mixture of magic and practical psychology. His mind seems to be unusually perceptive to people's emotional problems. By studying textbooks on nursing, he has picked up a knowledge of the human body that is quite considerable for a layman. Eduardo is not hostile to modern medicine. On the contrary, once he has determined that a client's pain results from a diseased organ or an injury, he suggests a clinic or hospital, hoping that poverty will not make this impossible.

But Eduardo has his own ways of helping. He is credited with locating lost objects which are of special value to the owner and also with foreseeing the outcome of important steps his client wants to take. But people primarily come to him from many miles away in the hope that he will ease the strain of harsh living conditions and lift off their minds, at least temporarily, the burdens of guilt, frustration, lack of success, and personal tragedy.

Night has fallen and the curandero's simple house is filled with people. Among them is a woman, young yet, but haggard and shapeless from too many childbirths and an insufficient diet. She complains about incessant headaches and stomach cramps.

First Eduardo takes a protesting live guinea pig from a cramped cage and rubs the small animal over the forehead and abdomen of the woman. When done right and accompanied by the properly chanted words, this ritual should transfer the ailment from the patient to the animal. This idea of transference crops up all through the ages. It has even found its way into modern psychiatry, where it stands for the emotional attachment of the patient to the psychiatrist.

In the case of the woman, the transference ritual has no effect. Therefore, stronger methods are called for. Obviously the pains are due to hostile witchcraft. Eduardo turns to the *mesa*, the ritual table on which has been placed an array of objects, among them a crucifix. There are also several swords and long staffs set beside some bowls and cups. They are reminders of a dim pagan past.

First a brew is prepared from a mixture of cactus and black tobacco juice. It is drunk not by the patient, but by the healer and his two young assistants. Under the impact of what must be a potent psychedelic drug, they launch into a drama-like session that may last until daybreak. Chants and prayers to the God of Christianity alternate with the shaking of the objects on the mesa. At one point, the curandero grabs a sword with each hand and lunges ferociously at an unseen enemy.

The session ends in the utter exhaustion of the performers, as well as the onlookers. The patient however, seems to have forgotten all about her pain.

Curanderos still ply their trade all over the pueblos of Latin America. Some have absorbed greater amounts of scientific knowledge than others. Many are familiar with a large quantity of useful herbs and other traditional home remedies. In many instances, they bring genuine relief, but when sweet basil is prescribed for the wife in the hope that it will bring back her straying husband, only despair makes her accept the advice.

The Catholic Church is not exactly happy with this combination of Christian and pagan activities. When the Europeans first conquered the country, curanderos were severely persecuted. But now they are mostly left alone. Church leaders recognize that they are rendering a service to the masses that nobody else is willing or equipped to give.

A Mexican mother brought her child to the local curandero. She was sure that a neighbor had cast a *mal ojo* (evil eye) on the little one. After looking the child over carefully, the curandero gave the following advice: "First say a prayer to the holy Mother of God. Then break an egg in a cup. Add small pieces from an old broom and then brush the whole body of the child with the stuff. This will make the *mal ojo* powerless." The mother went away with her mind at peace.

Another patient, an old man, was sure that the limp in his right leg had been hexed on him by a fellow to whom he had denied the hand of his daughter. He too was counseled to pray and then to throw dust in the direction of the offender's residence.

Kamuti Muthungi practices in Kenya on the east coast of Africa. He is a "traditional" doctor as distinguished from the "European" doctor who practices advanced scientific techniques in the hospital nearby. Muthungi knows his people thoroughly. He has lived among them all his life and so have his ancestors. This background gives him an understanding of his neighbors' feelings and longings, their fears and expectations. Unlike the "European" doctor, he is easily accessible. Muthungi takes his time talking with his visitors. His ceremonial healing acts are performed at a leisurely pace. He charges very little, which attracts many blacks and occasionally whites.

A woman has come into the simple consulting room leading a little boy by the hand. The child whimpers in constant pain. The healer listens patiently to the frantic pleas for help. He asks many questions to get the complete picture. Then he leans back and shakes a bunch of dried leaves that he holds in his right hand. The leaves crackle. Dust escapes from them as they swing back and forth. Muthungi's eyes close. Nothing moves in the room except his right hand with the short twigs covered with leaves.

He meditates for a long time. His mind tries to fit together the pieces. What similar cases has he encountered in the past? What medicine and which rituals have been successful, and where have he and other medicine men failed? A final conclusion escapes him. Still deep in thought, he reaches for a long, thin-stringed instrument that has been lying by his side. He plucks the strings and hums softly in a plea to forces beyond the room for guidance.

Finally, he comes to a decision. Here is the answer to the problem before him. "Take this antelope horn," he tells the mother. "Touch the child's chest with it when he cries and say: 'Pain, go away. The doctor said so.' "

The woman is disappointed. Clearly she had expected more immediate help. Muthungi, sensing the visitor's frustration, is ready for a second measure to back up the first. In a small cauldron, he grinds together pieces of bark, roots, leaves, and flower petals. The concoction simmers over the fire; he stirs it from time to time with a ladle of dark wood. The child is made to swallow some of the thick liquid. Soon he is asleep.

It is doubtful whether Muthungi has ever heard the term *placebo* (Latin for "I shall please"). It is well known to every modern physician. Many times a patient comes to the clinic complaining of some pain that would go away after a time without any medication. But for his money, the client expects to receive, if nothing else, at least a prescription for medication. It may call for a few pills that have no effect other than satisfying the patient's expectations. He is happy, just as the child's mother is happy with Muthungi's medicine. They both have received what they came for.

While the physician has to stick to pills, salves, and drops, the traditional healer can also prescribe charms of metal, wood, horn, or tooth to be worn around various parts of the body.

The child who was brought to Muthungi will be all right in a few days. In the rare instances where the patient returns, the healer has to apply stronger measures. He makes the ailing person stretch out on a mat and massages the body from head to toe. If nothing else, this brings about relaxation and increased comfort.

Though Muthungi believes in a supreme God, he does not exclude friendly and malevolent spirits from his universe.

When pain and discomfort persist despite various efforts, he believes it must be the work of an evil spirit, a stubborn and persistent sort of devil. The strongest guns in the healer's arsenal must now be readied for action to get rid of the spirit.

While his apprentice throws things into the fire to make a heavy bluish smoke, Muthungi breaks into a threatening chant. He bends over a sick man and taps all over his body to find the exact spot of the spirit's entry. A wound, a mole, or a wart will do. He punches and kneads this spot while intoning menacingly: "I order you to leave this patient at once."

This may or may not work. Given the healer's often practiced, intense gift of suggestion and the patient's desire to improve, however, it does have a good chance of succeeding.

Like that of his forebears, Muthungi's practice is not restricted to the aches of the body. His visitors lay before him their financial and sexual problems, too. He also gives advice when the whole community is pondering an important decision. He is always available, yet he remains a mysterious figure. Anybody who dared to lay hands on his tools or steal any of his secrets would leave himself open to the most frightening curses.

The tools and methods of contemporary witch doctors vary greatly from place to place. On the Gold Coast of Africa, folk healers impress their clients with their planned sloppy appearance. They go about wrapped in untidy garments, their hair unkempt and uncut. Wound around their necks are long strands of beads. The male healer wears a linen cap that was once white. His face is painted in grotesque colors with dark circles around the eyes. He carries a four-foot-long wand that is smeared with raw eggs. Pieces of eggshell adhere to the sticky mess. To scare away the demons, he discards his garments except for a short grass skirt that will not limit his movements when he launches into a wild dance.

A certain African witch doctor has a particularly ingenious way of treating toothaches. The name of the sufferer is written on a piece of paper. Then a needle is heated until the point glows red-hot. The needle is thrust through each of the letters that make up the name. This direct attack is supposed to kill instantly whatever caused the pain.

Lots of ingenuity is also expended on the concoction of folk medicines. Some may strike us as less than tasty, such as a mixture of horse dung and wine which is popular with a few African healers.

When we talk about folk healers of today, we must not forget the practitioners of *voodoo*. The term evokes images of frenzied dancing and ecstatic feats. Drums beat incessantly until the participants, under the spell of the enervating monotonous sounds, contort their bodies into impossible looking positions. Sometimes their dancing becomes very sensual. In such a state, they lose their normal fear of danger. Voodoo dancers grasp red-hot metal bars and step on burning logs with bare feet. It is often hard to distinguish whether a voodooist is in a true trance or just performing a clever act of showmanship.

Voodoo is still practiced, sometimes in secret, all over the West Indies, and particularly in Haiti, the most impoverished of the Caribbean islands. Voodoo is derived from old African religious customs brought along by slaves hundreds of years ago. In the New World it became overlaid with Christian—particularly Catholic—trappings.

In voodoo thinking, illness and death are of magical origin. Persons of evil intentions put spells on their victims. Sometimes puppets symbolizing the enemy are pierced with needles. People who learn that they have been cursed with a death spell have been known to actually waste away and die in a short time.

The treatment for this consists of countermagic in the form of endless prayers, sacrifices of animals, and appeals to friendly spirits. For the voodoo believer, there is no incurable illness. For every misfortune caused by magic there is a countermagic. Even better than countermagic is the prevention of evil magic by wearing amulets, ornaments worn as a charm against evil. An example of an amulet would be a copper wire worn around the wrist to keep away rheumatism. Powders and ointments to counteract spells are most potent when prepared on Christmas night.

The voodoo priest, the *houngan*, doubles as healer, especially for afflictions of the mind. He is the poor man's psychiatrist. In his *houmfar*, the voodoo temple, he performs his rites, often for a stiff price which his flock can ill afford.

When relatives bring him a man or woman who is completely insane, the houngan may alternate beating a drum with beating the sick person with a vicious-looking whip. One such practitioner whips his babbling patients seven times near an outdoor fire. It is a ritual whipping to chase away demons, but it still hurts. No wonder the poor patients try to run away. When this happens, the houngan puts them in handcuffs and leg irons. Shocking? Certainly, but it is well to remember that until quite recently that was the standard treatment for the emotionally disturbed in the "civilized" countries of Europe and America.

A strong stevedore wasted away within a few days to a mere skeleton barely able to stand on his feet. The houngan diagnosed a potent death spell. To counteract it, he splashed a brownish liquid into the patient's face. His body was showered with water, massaged, and then rubbed with oil, all under constant loud incantations. A trench was dug in the yard and a chicken was buried alive there. It was a trade-off:

the chicken's life for the man's. It worked. The sick man recovered speedily and was soon back to work.

To cure a baby from fever and diarrhea, the houngan instructed the mother to go into the street at five in the morning with seven cents. She was to hand a cent each to seven beggars without saying a word. The baby recovered after three such treatments, costing the mother twenty-one cents plus the houngan's fee.

Voodoo flourishes because people are miserable. Poverty and political oppression combine with widespread malaria, tuberculosis, and hookworm to drive the suffering to the voodoo priests from whom they expect comfort which no one else is prepared to give.

CHAPTER FOUR

Healing Shrines

THE PATH TO EPIDAURUS is steep and rocky. From the coastal town on the deep blue Aegean Sea where they had disembarked, the people hobbled the endless eight miles to the sacred groves. Many moved haltingly on crutches, others rode swaying on stolid donkeys. Softly moaning, they picked their way through clumps of crooked-stemmed olive trees and small terraced vineyards. Grazing sheep gave them a quick disinterested glance, but out of the whitewashed houses of the tiny villages women came with earthen jugs of water to refresh the travelers.

The caravan plodded along, a picture of misery. Yet hope shone in the eyes of those who could see, and even the faces of the blind were alight with expectation. After a strenuous sea voyage from their homes on the Dodecanese archipelago, they were now on the last lap of their journey to the shrine of Asclepius, the god of healing.

These were not crude Stone Age people. They were Greeks. About 2400 years ago, their civilization reached a peak so high and glorious that even in later centuries nothing could surpass it. In art and literature, in the training of the

43

body, and in the speculations of the mind, their accomplishments have remained models for humans to imitate right up to our own day.

While their illiterate forebears had feared and worshipped formless spirits of nature, the Greeks, with their vivid imagination, had created a whole community of gods dwelling on mist-shrouded Mount Olympus. Each god or goddess was a kind of divine specialist in such fields as fertility, war, commerce, seafaring, art, and so on. For every need, men and women had to turn to the proper god and worship that god in the right way.

The long line of wanderers struggled on—people with body pains, ones who had to be carried in litters, and others who babbled and raved and had to be restrained by their companions.

As the sun went down, the people reached the sacred place. There was a feeling of peace surrounding the courtyards in which fountains murmured and birds sang. Between tall cypress trees shone the white marble of low-slung buildings.

Priests in long loose garments approached in single file, softly chanting the god's praises. They welcomed the newcomers and then conducted them to the central courtyard which was dominated by the statue of Asclepius himself holding the symbol of his healing power, the staff with the snake coiled around it. Even today this is still the badge of the medical profession. In many societies snakes were held to be sacred. It was widely believed that wounds and sores would heal quickly when licked by nonpoisonous snakes. Under the god's feet gurgled a spring set in rose marble and decorated with mythical figures, half man and half beast.

The ailing drank from the spring. Then they were led to the edge of the central sanctuary of the healer-god. They did not enter, but were made comfortable on the portico which surrounded the building with the tall columns. After handing over to the priests the sacrificial gifts they had brought along for the god, they were served a sparse meal of strangely flavored dishes. The priests chanted a last prayer. The travelers washed by the fountain to purify themselves and then bedded down on couches to spend the mild Aegean night on the portico.

The priests had good reason to keep the patients out of the sanctuary during the first night. The god would not heal those who were already beyond help. If anyone was to die during the night, the decomposing body was not to defile the sacred interior. But the group had not come to die; they were filled with the hope to live.

When the first rays of the sun had begun to dry the dew of the night and to warm the guests, priests distributed white garments and then led the people into the temple itself. A careful questioning began.

"Has the god appeared to you in your sleep?"

"What did he reveal to you? Tell us exactly, so we can interpret his words for you, for we know well the ways of Asclepius."

Some of the people had been so keyed up that they had not slept at all. They were disappointed, but they were determined to try again the next night. Others had slept soundly without any dreams. But there were a few who reported having seen Asclepius in radiant clothing and heard him utter strange, incomprehensible words. Had they actually experienced the dreams, perhaps under the influence of certain drugs that were mixed into the evening meal? Or were they now imagining that they had seen the god in their dreams?

Whatever it was, the priests listened patiently and then made their comments. "This is what the god meant to convey. You should rest here for some days, drinking the water every few hours, eating sparingly, refraining from wine, but bathing and rubbing down your limbs frequently."

Many other pieces of sound advice were given in the name of the divine physician.

A few days later, many of the visitors felt refreshed and strengthened. They gladly gave Asclepias all the credit for the improvement. Before they left they had a priest engrave the story of their healing on a clay tablet. The temple walls were almost covered with testimonials in clay. When the next batch of ailing pilgrims read them, they would take comfort in what the god had done for others.

What was the secret of the shrine? Many explanations are given. For the ancient pilgrims of Epidaurus who were secure in their faith, it was the god who healed them. If they failed to get well, the fault lay with them. The modern researcher might argue that many a visitor felt his condition improved just because he firmly expected it to improve. It was *autosuggestion*. The priests, though not physicians in the modern sense, had accumulated much practical experience. Their advice was often sound and helpful. The atmosphere of peace and solemnity and the anticipation of miraculous events combined with rest and a good diet helped bring about a change for the better in the visitors, even though the relief was often only temporary.

Other ancient civilizations also made the temples of their gods into clinics and hospitals. Egyptians suffering from *melancholia*—what we would call depression today—were brought to temples and cheered with enchanting songs, entertaining games, and trips on the Nile River in gaily decorated boats.

Eventually the Hebrews replaced the multitude of gods with one all-powerful divine being. Christianity and Islam continued the idea of monotheism. There was no more room for a god of healing or for a sanctuary dedicated to him.

But new shrines came into existence and new generations of pilgrims sought them out. The ailing, as well as the poor, the barren, and the persecuted, kept on hoping that in such places their fervent prayers would have a better chance of being heard and answered than at home. For Christians this meant a visit to a church or monastery, but not just to any such consecrated spot. They went to special ones which had reputed records of miraculous cures. Pilgrims came singly or in large organized groups, traveling either distances of a few short miles or crossing wild alpine passes and stormy oceans. Many lives were lost along the way.

On the Greek island of Rhodes there are many tiny chapels built in the style of the Greek Orthodox branch of Christianity. Some stand far away from the villages on the crowns of steep hills. Inside the simple whitewashed structures, amidst clusters of thin burning candles and smoke-darkened icons, hang hundreds of small toy-like objects; some are of silver, but most are of a cheaper metal. They are crude replicas of arms, legs, eyes, and whole babies. Devout peasants brought them in gratitude for an ailment cured or for fertility restored —by God's direct intervention, they believe.

In earlier times the conviction that certain saints could cure certain diseases was widespread among Catholics. Saint Blasius was beseeched to relieve throat ailments, Saint Kilian to help with eye troubles, Saint Macarius to soothe persistent headaches, Saint Gervasius to cure rheumatism, Saint Apolonia to remove toothaches, and Saint Vitus to quiet convulsions and spasms. A nervous disease causing jerky movements of the body is still called Saint Vitus Dance. Theologically speaking, the saints are asked by the worshippers to plead for them with God, but in popular belief the saint himself often becomes a kind of spiritualized medical specialist.

The people still come in great numbers to pray in churches and basilicas dedicated to such a saint. In many instances the sanctuary contains the saint's tomb or a part of his body. The belief in the healing power of such relics has frequently been abused by swindlers. They have sold to churches splinters of the "true cross" and droplets that were variously described as the blood of Jesus, or tears, or even the milk of the Virgin Mary. Whether genuine or fake, as long as the petitioner believed in the effectiveness of the relic, it was bound to be credited with at least an occasional cure.

The arrival of scientific medicine did not stop the pilgrimages to healing shrines. People go because they have not yet learned to trust the trained physician or they cannot afford one. Then there are those who have been told by the physician that no cure exists yet for their ailment, that their case is hopeless.

Some healing shrines are known only in the immediate neighborhood; others draw pilgrims from all over the world. El Santuario de Chimayo is a little adobe church in New Mexico. Over five thousand hopeful supplicants assemble there on Good Friday. Many try to scrape off some of the adobe sand and take it with them; it is rumored to have healing qualities.

In Canada, near the city of Quebec, is the church of Sainte Anne de Beaux Prés. It houses hundreds of braces, crutches, and artificial limbs abandoned by happy pilgrims who decided that they had no more use for them. Outside the church a noisy carnival-like atmosphere reigns, complete with street hawkers and garish neon signs that advertise motels and eating places. Many regret deeply the commercialization of the spot which they hold sacred.

To visit the most famous of all healing shrines, one must travel to Lourdes, once a sleepy village in southern France near the Pyrenees mountain range. There Bernadette Soubirous, a simple peasant girl, startled villagers in 1858 with accounts of a series of visions. The Virgin Mary—Bernadette only referred to her as "The Lady"—ordered her to dig in the ground of a grotto by the side of a river. A spring gushed forth, and it has been flowing ever since. The girl later became a Catholic nun and died young. She has since been canonized as a saint.

As soon as word got out about the new spring, pilgrims began to flock to Lourdes. Reports of miracle cures swelled the trickle to a mighty stream. The original sleepy habitation of dirt-poor peasants is not recognizable anymore. Rows of hotels line the streets. Large hospitals stand ready to receive the infirm who come by train, bus, and private car or who are flown in by plane from other countries in Europe and beyond. The spring is now protected by a metal grill. The water collects in an artificial pool. Above the grotto stands a magnificent cathedral.

In the crowded streets, curiosity-hungry tourists mingle day and night with the sick who are able to walk. Those who are not so fortunate are pushed through the throng in ricksha-like carts with small canopies. At night lighted torches are carried in procession to the grotto where the blind, the crippled, and the leprous step or are carried into the ice-cold water. Some fill cups with the precious liquid and drink it. A statue of the Madonna, surrounded by hundreds of lighted tapers, looks down on the scene.

In the afternoon human misery waits in a huge assembly on a platform facing the cathedral. The carts with the bedridden are drawn up in a semicircle. Behind them stand those who have the use of their legs. An air of anticipation pervades the gathering.

The great church bells boom. A solemn procession approaches the plaza, led by a uniformed brass band marching slowly and playing the tune of a well-known hymn. Young girls in blue capes follow holding little bouquets of flowers in their folded hands. Behind them march priests in white surplices, and then a long line of acolytes carrying banners, lighted candles, and crucifixes. Several bishops in purple robes precede the golden canopy held high by four dignitaries in black morning coats. Under the canopy strides the officiating prelate clad in white and gold and carrying the golden monstrance that contains the host. Monks and nuns in the various habits of their orders, nurses in white uniforms, and several rows of doctors bring up the rear.

Under the golden canopy, accompanied by a rousing chorus and by the tinkling of tiny bells, the archbishop celebrates high mass. Mounting excitement grips the thousands of witnesses. Those who can, kneel devoutly as the celebrant raises the host high and traces with it the sign of the cross. The prayerful silence is broken by hoarse shouts:

"Lord, grant me to see!"

"Lord, grant me to walk!"

Others beat their breasts with weak fists. Tear-stained faces are lifted toward the improvised altar.

As the procession forms to make its way back into the basilica, a woman slowly and painfully raises her wasted body out of a wheelchair. Behind her an experienced orderly stands ready with outstretched arms to catch her. She makes several awkward steps with grotesquely swollen legs. "Look, I can walk," she shouts. "I haven't walked in ten years."

The crowd turns hysterical. The mass excitement could easily cause a deadly stampede, but a group of attendants, wise in the ways of emotional throngs, intones a well-known psalm. The moment of danger passes. With the ardor of exultation, the song wells up into the early evening. The crowd is convinced that a miracle has again occurred at Lourdes.

The pilgrims need no further proof, but the church authorities are not yet satisfied. Catholicism teaches that God in His unlimited power can indeed perform miracles, acts that defy the proven laws of nature. He has done so repeatedly, according to Biblical and church doctrine. He has awakened the dead to new life and has made incurable diseases suddenly disappear.

But the church very carefully checks up on each claim of a miraculous cure before it puts its stamp of approval on it. Every such claim is brought before a special commission of physicians, the *Bureau des Constations Médicales de Lourdes*. The doctors decide whether the affliction should be considered incurable according to present medical knowledge and whether the cure was sudden and complete. Before they make a final decision, they have the patient return to Lourdes in a year to make certain that he has been healed permanently. Only then does the commission give its approval, but the last word is always with the bishop of the patient's home district.

About two million pilgrims throng the streets and grotto of Lourdes each year. Yet within the first one hundred years since Bernadette's visions, only fifty cures have been declared miraculous by the church. They include the healing of blindness, cancer, and tuberculosis, which until recently was the main killer of men in European cities.

Even so, not everybody is convinced that those documented cures have been brought about by supernatural power. What about the millions of suffering beings who dragged themselves to Lourdes, with great personal sacrifice, only to return home more miserable than they were before? Were they all less deserving of God's grace than the select fifty? These are hard questions to answer. Doubters also question the impartiality of the medical commission and of the church authorities. They argue that even where a sudden cure has occurred, there must be a natural reason for it, although we may not yet have discovered it. Some people speculate that the strong emotional experiences at the shrine make symptoms of disease disappear, at least for a while. A physician who had directed pilgrimages to Lourdes for twelve years reported that no patient of his was ever cured, but that they went away with a new attitude of untroubled serenity.

The argument goes on. Whatever the judgment of those possessed with knowledge and authority, the people who suffer and who are desperate want to believe in miracles. They keep on going to Lourdes and other such shrines.

CHAPTER FIVE

Faith Healers

GODS DESTROY; gods also heal and restore life. We learn this from the myths of ancient peoples.

The Egyptians worshipped Osiris, god of the life-giving sun and of the river Nile which brought nourishing waters to the fields. As the legends tell it, he was married to the goddess Isis, who was also his sister. They had a brother named Set who was mean and jealous. One day he killed Osiris. But this is not the end of the story.

Set thrust the body of his dead brother into a casket and had it thrown into the Nile. It was swept far out to sea. Isis, the faithful wife and sister, set out to find the body, and when she did, she changed into a bird. As she hovered close above her slain husband, she flapped her wings vigorously. This caused a gentle, life-giving breeze. The slain god rose from the sea, and the loving couple was reunited. Set, the villain god, received his deserved punishment.

Similar myths were told by Assyrians, Babylonians, Greeks, and others. When the Hebrews proclaimed the reign of the one and only God, they taught that His power was limitless. He could restore life and health if He so decided, but in the Old Testament, the Bible of the Jews, He prefers to have such miracles performed through the acts of mortal men whom

He selects. The Book of Kings tells how a captain of the Syrian army was stricken with the dreaded curse of leprosy for which there was no known remedy. Through a captive he learned of the prophet Elisha who lived in Israel. So "he came with his horses and with his chariot and stood at the door of Elisha. And Elisha sent a messenger unto him saying, 'Go and wash in the Jordan seven times, and thy flesh shall come again to three and thou shalt be clean.'" The Bible continues to tell how the captain, after some reluctance, finally followed the advice and was indeed completely cured.

Two hundred years ago, a sect called the *Hassidim* came into being in Eastern Europe. These pious Jews were convinced that their local leader, the *rebbe*, could work miracles like the prophets of old, because of his spiritual closeness to God. When there was sickness they came to him to ask for his intercession with the Almighty. Even on the graves of dead rebbes, requests for help were left on slips of paper.

Miracles of healing are prominent in the New Testament. The Gospels tell in various passages how Jesus healed the sick and revived the dead.

> And when the men of that place had knowledge of him, they sent out into that country round about and brought unto him all that were diseased. And besought him that they might only touch the hem of his garment, and as many as touched were made perfectly whole. (Matt. 14)
>
> And great multitudes came unto him, having with them those that were lame, blind, dumb, maimed and many others, and cast them down at Jesus' feet, and he healed them. (Matt. 15)

Christianity teaches that the Master passed on His authority to the leading disciples. Peter and Paul performed healing miracles, and they were followed by the long line of saints. Particularly such well-known figures as Saint Patrick and

Saint Bernard are credited with healings which transcend the powers of nature. According to Catholic theology, to every saint is attributed at least one miraculous feat; many such accomplishments have to do with the healing of illness.

Ever since those distant days, men and women in pain have turned to persons who, it was said, had been granted the special gift of instant healing. Skeptics wondered why God should have selected people who seemed no better or more knowledgeable than many others. But those who suffered did not ask many questions. They clung to every straw of hope. In huge multitudes they sought out the healer, making him, at times, world famous and rich.

Faith healers, as they are commonly called, prescribe no medication and perform no operations. Most of them have never received any kind of medical training. They require no blood tests or urine specimens from their clients, only faith in *their* ability, conferred by God, to conquer illness.

The centuries have seen faith healers of many different kinds. Some were male, some female. Some were old, others still children; some lived in luxury, others in stark poverty. There were those who became superstars of faith healing, performing in huge assemblies with flamboyance and theatrical expertise. Others lived very humble lives, and the ailing had to make strenuous trips to reach them.

Brother Jonathan's abode was a dilapidated houseboat on the Mississippi River near New Orleans. He was already an old man when rumors spread in the 1920s that he had cured several persons who were on the verge of death. Soon thousands came down the muddy river bank and over the rickety gangplank to have Brother Jonathan lay his hands on their foreheads.

He was a simple soul whose desire to help was sincere, and he demanded no payment. The city health department did not like what was going on, but was reluctant to arouse the wrath of all the citizens who sought out the healer. Feeling that it ought to do something, the department ordered Brother Jonathan to wash his hands each time before touching a patient. He complied, and continued his work of love until he collapsed from exhaustion. The visitors went away feeling improved, and the more they told others about it, the better they felt.

In at least one case the gift of faith healing came to a man after his death. Father Powers had been a simple Catholic priest, hardly known beyond his parish in Malden, Massachusetts. But when he had departed from the earth in 1869, people told of having been cured of 'all sorts of ailments following a visit to the good Father's grave. The newspapers picked up the story, and the rush was on. Within three weeks 847,000 visitors stormed the cemetery and made a shambles of all the graves that had lain in peace for decades. On once well-tended flower beds and lawns lay heaps of discarded crutches and braces. Eventually, to stop a public nuisance and prevent scandal, the church authorities closed the whole cemetery. That ended Father Powers's faith healing from the grave.

The deceased priest was not present at his healings, at least not in the flesh. Living faith healers occasionally attempt something along the same line. To clients who live far away, they send specially blessed handkerchiefs through the mail.

More colorful, vibrant, and impressive are the revival meetings that combine emotionally charged worship with faith healing. Most of the groups which stage such multipurpose gatherings are stoutly conservative Protestants, such as the Pentecostals. Since they feel that Christ is present in their sessions as if He were a living person, miracles can and will occur at such times. But even then, it takes a specially chosen person to be the instrument of supernatural action.

Though medicine has, until very recently, been an almost

exclusively male profession, women became prominent as nonmedical healers. Nobody, male or female, ever outdid Aimee Semple McPherson when it came to impressive theatrical showmanship. The attractive evangelist possessed charm and a ready wit. Even the whiff of scandal that surrounded the thrice-married Aimee added to her popularity. Her revival meetings at Angelus Temple in Los Angeles and her numerous guest appearances elsewhere were well-orchestrated spectacles, and she always made sure that they received wide press coverage.

Thousands came to be healed by her. More than once, riots were barely prevented as masses of excited people pushed and shoved to get within touching distance of Mrs. McPherson. In San Diego the sessions had to be moved to Balboa Park since no hall could hold the gigantic crowds. The event lasted two days from early morning to dusk. The sick kept on coming and passing before her. In the end she fainted from exhaustion and had to be carried back to her hotel.

Her typical healing stance was to stand erect with one hand resting on the head of the kneeling patient and the other arm stretched up high in the air. Her eyes were closed in prayer. "Jesus is the healer," she declared. "I am only the office girl who opens the door and says, 'Come in.'" Ironically, this woman, praised by untold numbers of thankful followers for having freed them from illness, died in 1944 from an overdose of sleeping pills.

Aimee Semple McPherson is dead, but Oral Roberts is very much alive. It was Oral Roberts who made faith healing a household word. He became known to millions all over the world thanks to very professionally arranged preaching visits. His audience became even larger when he adopted the use of a new technological marvel, television.

What first directed Oral Roberts toward the path of healing was a personal experience. At the age of sixteen he contracted tuberculosis. But he claims that the illness suddenly disappeared while he was attending a revival service held by an itinerant Pentecostal preacher.

After his fame had been established, there was no church building in any city that could hold all the people who wanted to come and hear him. The largest meeting halls or auditoriums available had to be engaged. People came from more than fifty miles away. Wheelchairs were pushed through the aisles. The partially paralyzed hobbled to their seats holding on to the arms of companions.

The service got under way in the usual Pentecostal fashion: rollicking gospel hymns sung by a large choir, clapping hands and stomping feet heard all through the auditorium, the introduction of sponsoring local ministers, and the collection, handled by skillful ushers who passed large plastic buckets down the long rows.

When the crowd reached a high peak of emotion, the Reverend Roberts himself stepped to the microphone to deliver a fiery sermon in the true evangelical style. It was punctuated by frequent shouts of "Hallelujah" and "Praise the Lord" rising from the tightly packed crowd.

Finally, the evangelist invited the sick to come forward. They formed a long line all through the center aisle. Assistants helped them to mount the platform where Oral Roberts was sitting on a chair. He had taken off his jacket and rolled up his shirtsleeves, ready for action.

"What hurts you, brother (sister)?" he inquired. Whether the pains came from the head, the chest, or the stomach, the next question was: "Do you believe that the Lord Jesus Christ can heal you?"

When the answer was in the affirmative, as it always was, Roberts placed both hands on the petitioner's head, giving it a sudden violent shake while exclaiming in a commanding voice: "In the name of the Father, the Son and the Holy Ghost, be healed."

The assistants led the patient away to make room for the next in line. Some left dejected, more forlorn in their misery than when they had entered. But others shouted with tears streaming down their cheeks. "My pains are gone!" "I can see!" "I can walk!"

Their ecstasy spread to the spectators who broke into shouts of praise with arms raised and bodies swaying.

In his books, Oral Roberts describes a number of startling success stories. A woman with a spinal block that confined her to a wheelchair came to him. He placed his hands on her brow and "in the flash of a second, the healing power of God swept through her body, which began to tingle with life. The numbness and paralysis left her side ... and she jumped out of her chair and stood with her hands upraised, praising and magnifying God."

In 1968 Oral Roberts gave up his faith healing activities, but he still appears on national television to present religious messages. He is also the founder of Oral Roberts University and functions as its president.

Since his retirement, and before her death in March 1976, Kathryn Kuhlman could have been nominated as the number one faith healing star without encountering much opposition. Her charisma was a reminder of Aimee Semple McPherson, her fame was nationwide and durable. The length of Miss Kuhlman's ministry had passed the quarter century mark. She knew and mastered all the stage effects that could have possibly enhanced her presentation. Her timing was perfect. Before she made her entrance, the listeners had already been treated to the sweet strains of the organ, to the mellow baritone of the gospel singer, and to the powerful sounds of the four-hundred-voice choir.

At just the right moment, Kathryn Kuhlman appeared in flowing robes and gold slippers. Her face radiated joy as she expressed hope that many would be healed tonight. But a few minutes later, she would sob loudly for those who would not be so lucky.

In a giant auditorium healing could take place without the healer even being close to the afflicted person. With eyes closed and arms outstretched, she exclaimed, "There is a man over in the balcony—bursitis—it is gone." A little later she cried, "Somebody in the fourth row has just been cured of his spinal injury." To a girl who sat dejected in a wheelchair, she called in an imperious tone, "Walk, walk, I say. I rebuke your multiple sclerosis." The girl hoisted herself to her feet with tears streaming down her cheeks. This would continue until Miss Kuhlman exclaimed: "If you have been healed tonight, come to the stage and give praise to the Holy Spirit." The enraptured procession formed and made its way forward in an uproar of joy.

Kathryn Kuhlman proudly admitted that she knew nothing of medicine or therapy. When asked how she explained her gift, she answered with appropriate quotes from the Bible. In her appearances she took the direct approach in calling for hefty contributions. "I want twenty one-hundred-dollar checks," she would call, "so we can continue the Lord's work." But her assistants also accepted smaller amounts.

In her weekly television talk shows, followers gave testimonials about their cures. A war veteran whose spine had been injured in battle had worn back braces for twenty-three years and had been in constant pain. He told how he was completely healed during one of Kathryn's "miracle services" in Memphis, Tennessee. "When you said somebody was cured of spine trouble, I felt something like the sting of a needle in my back. I had the sensation of something hot entering my body. Then I jumped up to walk to the stage."

But there was also the woman who was "cured" of stomach cancer, but died four months after the "miracle service." Kathryn Kuhlman had her critics, but even they admitted that many persons suffering from hysterical disorders experienced a wholesome change of behavior after attending her services. Drug addicts had "kicked the habit," moved by the emotional experience. A girl was relieved of an embarrassing case of acne. (It should be remembered that this skin trouble, so common among young people, can have emotional roots.)

Aches, rashes, even lameness can disappear through a strong mental shock when they were caused in the first place by an irritation of the mind rather than the body. The tremendous uplift generated in many faith healing sessions can bring about a sense of peace which takes the place of worry about illness. It supplants pain and hopelessness with cheer. The miracle occurs, if for no other reason, because the sufferer wanted it to occur.

While observers from the medical profession are willing to admit all this, they still warn that reliance on faith healing can be not only useless, but also dangerous. By going this route, the sick person may lose valuable time in which to get proper medical treatment. By the time the patient turns to the physician it may be too late.

At times patients who were receiving medical treatment became impatient with the slow progress and turned to faith healers. Believing that they had been cured, they discarded the prescribed medication or injections, thereby sealing their doom. In his book, *Healing: A Doctor in Search of a Miracle*, Dr. William A. Nolan is very harsh in dealing with faith healers. After a lot of checking and interviewing, he came to the conclusion that many "healed" individuals actually got worse, and some died. But he admits finding that in a number of cases the symptoms of *psychosomatic* illness had disappeared.

A doctor who obviously had no great admiration for faith healers tried to strengthen his opinion by an experiment. At the time he had three very sick women patients. He told them: "I know a faith healer who is always very successful. I have asked him to pray for you tonight. He will ask God to cure you as he always does." The next morning all three patients reported that they felt very much improved even though the faith healer in question had never been told about them.

Such criticism does not turn away those who are desperate for comfort. The uneducated and unsophisticated are not the only ones to bypass the medical profession, although they are in the majority. In the prestigious Saint Bartholomew's Episcopal Church on New York City's Park Avenue, a group of businessmen, secretaries, and professionals from various fields assembles every Thursday at noon. Foregoing the many fashionable restaurants serving gourmet lunches around Manhattan, they hold a healing service almost next door to the most up-to-date clinics and hospitals in the world. The Episcopal Church of America is known to attract a membership which is not only financially well off, but also above average in formal education. It has always stressed dignity and decorum in its religious expressions. The Thursday meetings in Manhattan indicate that faith healing has begun to make inroads in various branches of "mainstream" Protestantism. One can now find some Lutheran and Methodist congregations that go in for it. Most of the enthusiasm, however, is still being generated within the Pentacostal and Evangelical groups.

There are faith healers who stay in one place while others roam from community to community. Many are known only to a small circle of believers while others rise to national and even international fame, assisted by a highly efficient public relations apparatus. Among the practitioners are those who are deeply convinced that God has chosen them for some unfathomable reason to be His tools. But there are also instances in which a clever huckster has pretended to do God's will while lining his pockets with the gifts of those in need of help.

The doubter asks: "If God wants to heal, why does he need Oral Roberts or Kathryn Kuhlman to assist Him?" Furthermore, why does a compassionate God allow pain and sickness to exist at all? If His power is unlimited as the spokesmen of religion proclaim, He could certainly do away with all such misery. These are profound questions. Theologians have wrestled with them for ages. But the masses that fill the halls when noted faith healers make their appearances are not bothered by such inquiries. Their beliefs are firm and free from doubts or reservations. What they bring with them is *faith*, and that makes faith healing possible.

~~~~~~

CHAPTER SIX

The Royal Touch

LONDONERS WERE OUT IN FORCE to cheer their king, Charles II. Less than two decades before, they had filled the streets to shout for his father's head, and the head of Charles I had indeed rolled into the dust, severed from the neck by the henchman's axe.

The gruesome execution of the British ruler had taken place in the middle of the seventeenth century. The English people wanted to try governing themselves without the absolute power of a crowned king, but the experiment did not work. After only a few years, many Britishers were ready to submit once more to the power of a king, even though the power had become severely reduced. They also wanted to enjoy once more the pageantry and the pomp that go with the existence of royal courts, and they received their fill of it when fun-loving Charles II assumed the vacant throne in 1660.

The bitter and violent arguments between king and parliament were forgotten now, at least for the moment.

The crowd had waited throughout the foggy morning to see their monarch pass. People waved from windows, with the more adventurous ones even climbing on rooftops to get a better view. It was the day of the King's Touch.

Heralds announced his approach with trumpets sounding.

Guards on horseback and soldiers armed with long staffs cleared an opening through the packed human mass. Councilors and clerics in splendid robes and gold chains followed. Finally the royal coach came in sight drawn by six matched horses with lavishly clad outriders and footmen. A band of pipers and drummers followed the carriage, but the sounds of their instruments were nearly drowned out by the clanging of all the church bells of London.

Surrounded by his court, the king ascended the broad steps to the great banquet hall of the city. The Lord Chamberlain conducted him to the throne that stood on a raised platform. At the foot, the sick waited in a long line. Before the ruler's arrival, doctors had carefully checked all the supplicants and turned away anybody they found unsuitable for the honor. Those who remained had been neatly scrubbed and combed by servant women. Now their faces were shining, cleansed by the water and colored by hope.

One by one, they stepped forward and fell on their knees. Charles, wearing the crown of England on his head and the ermine mantle of royalty over his shoulders, looked slightly bored. At times he had difficulty suppressing a yawn. But he was determined to go on with the ceremony. After what had happened to his father, it was extremely important that he impress the people with the majesty of his office.

While the royal chaplain was chanting passages from the Bible, the king reached out with both hands and let them glide slowly over the face of the shivering subject before him. At such a moment, the ailing British townsman or peasant at the king's feet would have remained frozen in his position, dazed by the splendor of the moment. But the chaplain nudged him with his big book, and when this failed to rouse the patient who was now supposed to be healed, hefty arms belonging to helmeted guardsmen lifted him into a standing position. Then he was handed a gold coin specially minted for the occasion. It was to be worn as an amulet to help make the king's cure a permanent one. No one has ever figured out how many Englishmen came to be healed and how many were mainly interested in receiving the coin.

While one invalid withdrew clutching his coin, convinced that the spell of illness had been broken, the next had already been positioned for the royal touch. Charles II supposedly "touched" about 92,000 persons during his reign of fifteen years. The statistics kept in the seventeenth century may not have been too accurate, but it must have been an impressive number. It is reported that one day the crowd of health-seekers was so great that six or seven of them were trampled to death. The royal touch did not extend to the power of reviving the dead.

The custom of the royal touch was a logical extension of the belief that God is the supreme healer. The crowning of a king was a solemn religious ceremony performed by the highest church dignitary. In the Middle Ages emperors were crowned by the Pope himself. It was strongly believed that in being anointed and consecrated by the church, the king assumed some sort of divine power. Rulers themselves tried to impress upon their people that they ruled in God's name and that any act of disobedience or disloyalty was tantamount to going against God's will. Defenders of the unrestricted power of the monarch spoke of the "divine right of kings." If the ruler acted as the representative of the Lord within a certain country, why should he not also possess the divine gift of healing? To be touched by His Majesty must surely have a very strong health-promoting effect.

The royal touch was practiced by the rulers of many countries. People came to them bleeding and feverish, with swollen limbs and bloated stomachs, and they all desperately wanted to believe in the king's ability to restore them to good health. It became known throughout the land that the king's touch was especially effective against one very common disease, a form of tuberculosis involving the painful swelling of the lymph glands in the neck. Known as *scrofula* and also as the King's disease, it was once a dreaded killer of people. During the reign of Charles II more persons died of the King's disease than at any other period of English history despite his frequently administered royal touch.

French kings practiced healing by touch all through the Middle Ages and on to the time of the great revolution which swept away all royal privileges, including the touch. Their English colleagues began to cure their subjects way back in the eleventh century when Edward the Confessor started "touching for the King's evil." Queen Elizabeth, who was shrewd and also somewhat stingy, decided that to spend the equivalent of $50,000 annually for healing medals was too much. She ordered the size of the gold amulets drastically reduced.

In order to receive the benefits of the royal touch, a nation has to have royalty. Between the rules of Charles I and Charles II (between 1649 and 1660), the British had no kings, only a dictator by the name of Oliver Cromwell. Apparently a mere dictator's touch cannot do as much good as that of a duly crowned king. A substitute toucher came forward, an Irishman by the name of Valentine Greatrakes. When he rubbed a sore arm or an aching abdomen with his fingers, the patient felt himself immediately relieved. So even though he wore neither crown nor scepter, unending throngs of suffering humanity came to him. He availed himself of neither pills nor bandages, only of the muscle power in his right arm. All over the country he was affectionately known as The Stroker. Only when the monarchy was reestablished did stroking again become a royal prerogative.

Eventually the spread of modern thought and scientific knowledge brought the custom of the royal touch to an end.

The philosopher David Hume stated that it was abandoned because "it could no longer give amusement even to the populace and was attended with ridicule in the eyes of all men of understanding."

King William III who succeeded Charles II must have shared Hume's sentiments. He still performed the royal touch to please his people. Once when he laid his hands on the brows of an ailing Englishman, he loudly pronounced the words which had been used by many kings before him, "May God give you better health;" he was then heard to add in a somewhat lower voice, "and more sense."

CHAPTER SEVEN

Driving Out the Devil

A YOUNG WOMAN lay trembling on a cot. The room was dark, the shutters were tightly closed. From time to time a groan escaped from her blue lips like the cry of a wounded animal. Her frightened relatives crowded in a corner.

Heavy velvet curtains parted and a priest strode forward clad in a long black robe. His outstretched arm held a large crucifix as if it were a sword in the hands of a fighter. With measured steps he advanced towards the writhing figure on the cot. "Servant of Satan," he thundered in Latin, "depart at once. Cease your devilish magic. I admonish you in the name of Jesus."

The girl choked. Froth formed at the corners of her mouth. The thin body shook violently. But the priest raised the wooden crucifix still higher. "I command you in the name of the Lord. Cease and depart."

Slowly he traced the sign of the cross over the prostrate figure, once, twice, a third time. An acolyte who had entered behind him swung a brass censer, and the air was filled with the sweet fragrance of incense.

Suddenly, the woman uttered an unearthly shriek. In terror her relatives withdrew even deeper into their corner, but the priest stood his ground, erect as a monument. Then the woman rose slowly from the cot, opened her eyes, and shook her head in bewildered surprise. Out of habit she genuflected before the priest whom she did not recognize. Then she fled into the arms of her shaken family. "Take me home," she urged. "I am so hungry and tired. I must have had a terrible dream, but I can't remember what it was."

This event occurred around the middle of the eighteenth century in the small Austrian village of Klosters. Father Johann Joseph Gassner had just performed the rite of *exorcism*.

The Catholic priest was a famous exorcist. It had all begun when he suffered from unbearable headaches that would not stop. He became convinced that the pain was the work of demons inside his body. After he performed the ancient rite of exorcism on himself the pain stopped. Word of his success got around. Soon parishioners came to him for help, then others who lived farther away. Encouraged by his new popularity, the Father took to traveling around Austria and neighboring Germany and Switzerland, carrying with him crucifix, vestments, and censer.

With his deep sonorous voice and the sureness of his bearing, he made a deep impression on his followers. He could order ranting, highly disturbed patients to quiet down and they would immediately obey. Others too weak to stand erect were commanded to walk. They rose with smiles on their lips and marched from the room.

Not everybody was favorably impressed by the exorcising cleric. Many who had come to him and were thought to be cured soon suffered relapses and ended up in worse shape than before. Also, the more exorcisms he performed, the more people came forward proclaiming that they were tormented by devils. Demonic possession turned into an epidemic. Church officials in Austria became so embarrassed that they finally forbade Gassner any further exorcising and made him stick to his duties as pastor and preacher. Soon he was just an obscure cleric again.

Exorcism is as old as humanity itself. We find it in the chants and dances of the preliterate shaman. When the later, more advanced civilizations made some of the spirits into gods, their adversaries were cast in the roles of demons or devils. Tibetan monks, Taoist priests in China, and Zoroastrian magi in Persia set themselves the task of ridding human bodies of those superhuman villains. The Gospel according to Mark tells of the lunatic who was bound in chains, but who continued to rant and rave and to break his chains. Whereupon Christ drove out the devils from this man's body and made them enter a herd of swine rooting nearby.

It was mainly the emotional or mental type of disease that was associated with the entry of invisible creatures into the human body. Such possessions were not always judged to be of an evil nature. Ancient Greeks and Hebrews sometimes looked at insane persons as divinely inspired. They were revered as seers or prophets, and clever priests tried to interpret their incoherent words to the flock as sound advice or as forecasts of future events.

The concept of the devil and his legions of hellish helpers originated in ancient Persia. There, about five centuries before Christ, Zoroaster taught that, unseen by human eyes, a fierce struggle goes on in the universe between the Master of light and goodness and his opponent, the ruler over darkness and evil. Both contend for the souls of mortals, and humans must take sides and choose whom they want to follow.

As soon as similar ideas were introduced into the Western religions, the lot of the insane became much more tragic. This is how it remained almost until our own days. Because their behavior offended the morals or religious feelings of the majority, or simply because they were thought to be strange and therefore threatening, these sick people were treated with shocking brutality. Everybody, including scholars and clerics, was convinced that only demonic possession could explain mental illness.

A hysterical person, for example, may laugh and cry for no apparent reason. Early Christian observers concluded that in this way demons expressed their contempt for devout Christian society. Demons were fallen angels. They had once rebelled against God and entered the services of His adversary, Satan. But there was hope that through prayer combined with certain ritual acts demons could be forced to abandon their victim. However, the forces of evil were expected to put up a bitter drawn-out struggle. Exorcism amounted to a contest between the representatives of the Lord and His enemies.

It was always considered a dangerous contest. The exorcist risked his life. Even when the demon was made to leave the sick, the danger was not yet over. The evil spirit could quickly find another victim, even the exorcist himself. That would make it an act of devilish vengeance. Therefore, the act of driving out Satan's emissaries remained extremely risky, even when successful.

In the first centuries of Christianity, the general pattern of exorcism was already set. The theologian Origen had the men or women he considered possessed by demons kneel before him. He drew the sign of the cross over the sufferer's head and sprinkled holy water over the brow. Then he intoned: "I exorcise thee, evil spirit, in the name of Jesus Christ. Tremble, o Satan, thou enemy of the faith, thou foe of mankind, thou root of all evil."

For a long time exorcism was the standard procedure applied to the mentally ill. Those unlucky people suffering from *schizophrenia* were especially singled out for the ritual. A schizophrenic person lives under the delusion that he is somebody else or that two or three or more different personalities inhabit his body at different times. Such individuals were immediately suspected of being possessed by one or several devils. On medieval manuscripts we can see pictures, drawn with child-like simplicity, showing a saint performing the exorcism on a demented creature. We see the evil spirit, usually depicted with horns and wings, leaving the patient. He emerges from the mouth, presumably flying back to hell from whence he came.

The phenomenon of the split personality figures in the Jewish legends about *dibbuks*, spirits of the dead which enter the bodies of living persons. One such legend has been made into a stage play and also into a musical. The scene is the ghetto, the Jewish quarter in a Russian town about two hundred years ago. A young, desperately poor follower of the Hassidic sect and the daughter of a wealthy merchant fall in love with each other. The merchant scorns the courtship of the indigent student and arranges a match for his daughter with a more suitable partner. The young Hassid dies of a broken heart and of excessive self-mortification. On the day of the wedding the bride-to-be suddenly begins to speak with the voice of her dead lover. His spirit, in the form of a dibbuk, has entered the girl's body. Led by the rabbi, the whole congregation proceeds to exorcise the dibbuk. Black candles are lighted in the synagogue, and the ram's horn is blown. Clad in his long prayer shawl and holding aloft the scroll of the *Torah*, the Five Books of Moses, the rabbi entreats the spirit to return to the grave of the dead student. At the climax of the tense rite, the girl regains her own personality, but seconds later she falls back lifeless, joining her sweetheart in the spirit world.

Many branches of Christianity have resorted to exorcism at one time or another. Pastor John Darrell built up quite a reputation in this endeavor shortly after the establishment of the Church of England in the sixteenth century. He was called to minister mostly to young women who disturbed family and neighbors by their fits, their moaning, and their offensive shrieking. Eventually, the Reverend Darrell was imprisoned, not so much for casting out devils as for doing it without the proper license from higher church officers. He was also suspected of fraud. His detractors charged that the whole performance of the hysteric fits followed by the successful exorcism was usually prearranged by the clergyman in collusion with his client.

When exorcism was not followed by the desired results, more cruel measures were devised. The purpose was to make things so uncomfortable for the demon inside the body that it would find it wiser to leave. To that end the miserable victims were flogged, chained, and prevented from sleeping. They were put on the block to be held up to public ridicule. Food was withheld from them presumably with the reasoning that, along with the patient, the devil inside him would also be left to starve.

This explains at least partially why the mentally ill have been treated for so long with almost unbelievable cruelty and neglect.

Within the Catholic Church the rites of exorcism were formalized centuries ago. The lengthy sequence of prayers and scriptural readings can be found in a volume entitled the *Roman Ritual*. In earlier times the book was used quite frequently. New converts were subjected to exorcism as a matter of course to cleanse them of pagan impurities. The method of driving out demons is taught as part of the training which candidates of the priesthood receive. At one point during their long schooling, they are officially granted the degree of exorcist. But no cleric is allowed to perform the ritual without permission from his superiors.

In recent decades the church has rarely resorted to exorcism. On the contrary, the higher authorities warn priests to be wary of overexcited parishioners who claim that they or their relatives are possessed. In such cases, the advice given is to seek out the help of medical experts, especially psychiatrists. They have, in most instances, been able to treat successfully patients with split personalities or women, among them nuns, who complained of being haunted and even sexually assaulted by devils.

But Catholic teaching does not rule out the existence of demons, just as it acknowledges, albeit with extreme caution, the possibility of miracle healings. Like other Christian groups, it holds that Satan exists. He or his devilish underlings may conceivably take over the body of an unhappy mortal. If, after thorough examination, no other explanation can be found for the emotional disorder, then exorcism is called for.

In the last three hundred years, the interference of angels, saints, spirits, devils, or demons in our daily lives has been widely questioned. With the rise of the natural sciences we became reluctant to deal with forces that are not controlled by natural laws. But in very recent times a reaction has set in. The younger generation especially has begun to feel that modern science and technology have created more problems than they have solved, that they are at least partially responsible for the looming dangers of pollution, overpopulation, and possible total destruction by nuclear war.

In 1971 the novel *The Exorcist*, by William P. Blatty, was published. What looked at first like just one more book among hundreds that hit the bookstores and paperback racks that year turned out to be an instant bestseller, and was made into a movie.

Mr. Blatty took the idea for his book from an actual event. A fourteen-year-old boy living in Maryland was reported to be possessed by the devil. He was relieved of his torment by an exorcism that lasted for over three months. In the novel the patient is a girl, the daughter of an agnostic actress. The child's personality is suddenly transformed into that of a monster. Her mouth utters the sounds of different voices, not only of humans, but also of animals. Her language becomes foul beyond belief, and everybody who comes near her is greeted with hate and abuse. Even her facial expressions change. Her new self seems to know facts that, at least according to her mother, she could not have known before. Her body wastes away, almost before the terrified eyes of those close to her. It emits a nauseating stench. In her room pieces of furniture move around and strange noises erupt that cannot be accounted for.

The mother makes the rounds of physicians, including specialists in neurology and psychiatry, but to no avail. Medical science succeeds in keeping the body alive with drugs and intravenous feeding, but it is helpless at getting to the root of the trouble.

In her desperation the mother approaches a priest who is also a fully trained psychiatrist. Though not a Catholic, she becomes convinced that only demonic possession can explain the horrible things afflicting her daughter, and she implores the cleric to perform an exorcism.

After a thorough medical and psychological examination of the girl, the priest reluctantly convinces himself that possession is the only explanation left. After receiving a bishop's permission, he secures the assistance of another priest, and together they begin the exercises of the Roman Ritual. Around the clock they recite prayers, chant psalms, and command the forces of evil to leave. At certain moments noted in the manual, their fingers draw the sign of the cross over the child's twisted features. Draped in cassocks and purple stoles and armed with a supply of holy water, they continue their efforts through the day, the following night, and into the next day. The two exorcists are at the end of their strength. At the climactic moment the unclean spirit is indeed forced out of the girl's body. It engages the priests in a fierce struggle which ends with the death of the Fathers and the flight of the demon. The girl is cured. She reverts to her original innocent self and remembers nothing of the frightening personality changes that have taken place.

Father John J. Nicola is not a character in a novel, but a real priest and an expert on the Catholic teachings concerning exorcism. As such, he acted as a consultant to the producers of the film. He reports that after the publication of the book and even more so after the release of the film, large numbers of people, mainly teenagers, came forward maintaining that they were possessed. The force of suggestion does strange things with people's imagination.

As the outsider looks at the process of exorcism and at what it sometimes accomplishes, he may, of course, affirm his faith in the existence of devils and in the power of the appropriate church officials to drive them out of human bodies. Or else he may accept an explanation more likely to be offered by a secular scientist: that the rite of exorcism works as a kind of emotional shock treatment. Throughout the lengthy process, the "possessed" person is given the extended attention he so strongly desires. The unfulfilled need of such attention could have had something to do with the origin of his trouble. The impressive ceremony conducted by persons held in high esteem is apt to open the patient's mind effectively to the power of suggestion. Following this line of thought, we can say that the evil spirit flees when the patient regains for himself the will to be healed.

CHAPTER EIGHT

Witches and Dancers

THE MARKETPLACE was as crowded as on the patron saint's day. This was a town in Germany with walls and gates, but it could just as well have been somewhere in France or Spain or any other European country.

Men had come with their wives and children. There was a holiday atmosphere. Baskets with food and drink were in evidence. The townspeople were prepared to settle down for a spectacle that they hoped would last for many hours. It was free entertainment, something to break the monotony of their eventless lives.

In the center of the plaza a high pile of dry wood was being prepared. From its top a single stake reached skyward. The town's executioner was standing by with a flaming torch in his hand.

"Here comes the witch!" people began to shout. Fathers raised toddlers high so that they could get a better look at the hapless creature who was now being dragged to the top of the brush pile. She was still a young girl, barely out of childhood. Her hair was disheveled, her face streaked with tears and caked dirt. She struggled feebly as strong hands tied her to the stake with stout rope.

The executioner touched the torch to the brush. The hushed crowd could hear the first crackling of burning wood.

The most radical way to deal with sickness is to kill those who are sick. To the shame of the human race, this was done thousands of times, and not only during the so-called Dark Ages. The practice of eliminating illness by eliminating the ill continued well through the most illustrious period of European history, the Renaissance of the fifteenth and sixteenth centuries. Here an enlightened intellectual minority was already celebrating the beauty of the human body and the greatness of the human mind in magnificent works of art and in scientific discoveries which completely changed the individual's picture of the world.

Medicine and the science of biology were making the first important steps in the direction of astounding modern accomplishments, yet the insane, especially when they were women, continued to be thought of as possessed by demons. The belief even spread, and more and more individuals were tagged with the deadly label of witch. Eventually there were so many of these people that the lengthy exorcising was replaced by the simpler and quicker method of putting the person to death—burning at the stake.

Highly educated scholars, among them prelates of the church, believed in the power of witches just as illiterate peasants did. In fact, it was an appeal by Pope Innocent VIII in 1488 that caused witch hunting to begin on a grand scale.

The victims were poor wretches who happened to act in odd ways. They were immediately accused of having made a voluntary contract with the devil. This pitiful group was made up of mentally retarded women, epileptics, and other people who suffered from delusions and hysteric seizures. Instead of receiving treatment, they were thrown into dungeons. Their tormentors tried to force confessions out of them. Jailers, judges, and confessors seriously believed that torture was a means to get at the truth. It is amazing how inventive the human mind can be when it comes to devising intricate methods of torture. Suspected witches were stretched on the rack, hung by their thumbs from beams, and burned with torches placed on their hands and at their feet. Thumb screws, pincers to pull nails, and water to fill stomachs were used in addition to whips, manacles, exposure to heat and cold, prolonged hunger, thirst, and sleeplessness.

Not surprisingly, those who survived the treatment confessed to anything they were asked about. Women admitted to casting spells on neighbors, causing death in childbirth or malformed babies. Together with the Jews and other persecuted groups, witches were accused of bringing about plagues. It was nearly always a woman who was singled out as a suspect due to the old prejudice that women were the root of all evil. A narrow-minded, but widespread interpretation of Genesis, the first book of the Bible, blamed Eve, the first woman, for having brought about man's sinfulness. It was Eve who caused us to lose the opportunity of spending all our days in paradise. Needless to say, this kind of interpretation was always made by males who sought a religious justification for treating women as inferiors. It was comforting to believe that men fell into sin because women tempted them, and not because of their own willingness. Therefore, the people saw a close connection between the female sex and the devil.

The penalty for admitted witchcraft was usually death, and the favorite form of dispatching such women to the nether world was burning them alive at the stake. The odor of roasting flesh could be smelled throughout Europe. When emigrants left the old continent for a new life in America, the witch-hunting craze crossed the Atlantic with them. In 1692 nineteen women were hanged as witches in Salem, Massachusetts. The noose replaced the stake in the Western Hemisphere.

It was not unheard-of that poor demented women voluntarily denounced themselves as witches. They practically pleaded to be persecuted. This mania of self-destruction is well-known to modern psychiatry. Every sensational crime story published in the media brings about numerous false self-accusations. Police stations are inundated with the confessions of disturbed persons who seek the limelight no matter what the consequences.

When the fear of witches reached epidemic proportions, it was the accusers rather than their victims who seemed to have lost their emotional balance. Everybody whose behavior was in any way unusual came under suspicion. Sometimes disaster could strike even those who never strayed from the norm. A malevolent neighbor could take revenge for a past slight. A debtor could get rid of his creditor, or a husband his wife through the convenient charge of witchcraft.

Greed and perverted lust motivated "witch pickers," who went about searching the bodies of suspect women for marks that were said to be seals of their pact with Satan. These were warts or other blemishes that would not bleed when pricked with needles or knives.

The most famous execution of a convicted witch was the public burning of Joan of Arc in the city of Rouen in 1431. During the Hundred Years' War between France and England, this French peasant girl appeared at the court of Charles VII, the heir to the throne of France, at a moment when he was about to lose the war completely. Joan's story was that several saints had repeatedly appeared to her and ordered her to come to the yet uncrowned king's aid. Charles was about to give up the struggle, but Joan persuaded him to continue the fight. She accompanied the soldiers into battle and, with her as their inspiration, they won a string of stunning victories. Charles VII was solemnly crowned king in the city of Rheims, which he had conquered through the leadership of Joan. However, in a later military campaign, she was captured by the British. The French king did nothing to exchange or ransom her despite the fact that he owed her his throne. That encouraged her captors to put an end to the woman who had shamed them on the battlefield.

It was easy to find an excuse for sending her to her doom. She claimed to have had visions which nobody else could perceive, she dressed in men's clothes, she bore arms, and she repeatedly led armies to victory. All this was very·strange behavior for a peasant girl. No wonder it was interpreted as proof of an unholy alliance with the devil. But the conviction by a high court of clerics and the terrible punishment only occurred after she had lost her usefulness to the French government. Earlier she had been hailed as a national heroine who acted under divine inspiration. Today, long after the ashes of her abused body have blown into the winds, her statue stands in every French city, the very embodiment of patriotism, and her name is on the roster of Catholic saints.

For a long time the belief in the existence of witchcraft was so common that neither kings nor cardinals denied it. Not until about two centuries after the death of Joan of Arc did the fires of fanaticism and mass hysteria begin to die down. A measure of tolerance and humanitarian compassion slowly asserted itself. Scientific medicine made a modest start, although the same doctors who were already aware of the true nature of biological man still believed in demons and witches. They were, after all, children of their times, and they could not immediately shed all the notions and prejudices they grew up with.

Witches still exist today in civilized countries. We know this because they say so without fear. They are neither being hunted down nor tortured nor burned at the stake anymore. In fact, together with other old practices, such as astrology, witchcraft is making a sort of comeback. Today's witches may be middle-class housewives, secretaries, or nurses. Though the majority is female, there is a sprinkling of men among them who call themselves *warlocks*.

Not even their enemies suspect contemporary witches of riding through the night on broomsticks to orgies with the devil. The *covens*, as small groups of witches are called, more closely resemble our familiar fraternal lodges. When witches gather, they engage in various secret rituals involving altars, torches, swords, and robes embroidered with mysterious signs. The favorite hours for the rites are between midnight and dawn. Today's witches assert that what they practice is pre-Christian religion. Their rites were performed more than two thousand years ago in the forest clearings of what are today England, France, and Germany.

When a witch writes or talks about her life or is being interviewed for a newspaper or television station, she invariably calls herself a "white witch." White witches strongly affirm that they use their knowledge and their psychic powers only for the good of people, and that goes particularly for their claimed ability to help the sick in mind and body.

Meeting a witch is very different from visiting the doctor's office down the street. As of old, she provides charms, pronounces magic formulas, and prescribes strange herbs to be taken at the time of the waning moon. Maintaining that she can see into the future, she may warn the visitor against undertaking a trip because she foresees an accident.

There are also "black witches," at least that is what the white ones maintain. The black variety is only out for mischief. They cast spells that make people sick or demented, and the white witches have their hands full trying to undo the evil work of the black ones.

The witchcraft mania of bygone centuries was a form of mass hysteria, and not the only one on record. Those outbreaks came in the wake of threatening dangers and catastrophes. In the thirteenth and fourteenth centuries, the Black Death stalked across the face of the European continent. This terrible epidemic almost emptied whole countries of their inhabitants. No remedy was known then that could have stopped the progress of what we now know to have been the bubonic plague. It had to run its course.

People desperately tried to halt the plague, but often, instead of preserving lives, their actions only made death come quicker. Since it was widely believed that the epidemic was God's punishment for man's sins, drastic forms of penance were devised. Groups formed in which people flogged each other and themselves while praying for mercy. Naked or in rags, they wandered across the countryside picking up recruits as they went along. Their state of complete physical exhaustion made them, of course, easy prey for the plague which they were trying to escape.

Witches were accused of participating in lewd dances, but not everybody who danced was called a witch. Dancing developed into a highly contagious hysterical movement without the vaunted association with Satan. People began to whirl in the streets and could not stop. Children and elderly people danced along highways until they collapsed, either dead or in a state of insanity.

Processions of dancers moved from town to town. In 1237 a large band of German children danced from Erfurt to Arnstadt. When the dancers entered a city, they halted in the central square. Forming a circle, they began to dance, first slowly, then faster and faster until finally their bodies were contorted and foam dripped from their mouths. The local townspeople first watched in bewilderment, but they were soon caught up in the frenzy and took the places of those who had dropped from complete exhaustion.

Dancing, like self flogging, was tried as a means to stop the plague. In 1418 big crowds danced day and night in Strasbourg, a city west of the Rhine river, in the hope that this would induce the Black Death to bypass the city.

The rhythmic movement of human bodies appeared not only to ward off disease, it could also serve as a cure, although with questionable results. In southern Italy it was believed that the dancing mania was caused by poison which entered the body from the bite of a spider, the *tarantula*, probably named after the city of Taranto. The poison made the victim squirm and twist in a very uncomfortable travesty of a dance. Far from restraining the dancing, the folk healers of the time even furnished the music. The sound of flutes, oboes, and drums was supposed to bring relief. By turning the uncontrolled squirming into a pleasant rhythmic motion, the power of the poison was supposedly diminished. So whenever a child reported having been bitten by a spider, the musicians were immediately called in. The fun of the music and the dance soon made the bitten child forget the pain and discomfort. This gave nature time to do the actual healing. (A certain lively type of musical composition is still called a *tarantella*.)

As the terrible plagues faded from the scene, the dancing mania also ebbed away. Dancing can lead to intense emotional excitement, especially when large numbers are involved. In our day, the frenzy generated by thousands of young people attending a rock concert demonstrates the power of mass suggestion heightened by throbbing rhythms and constant repetition. How much stronger than the impact of a rock festival must have been the old compulsion to dance that was brought about by the stark fear of death.

In our modern mental hospitals and clinics, patients are encouraged to dance, make music, and engage in other forms of artistic expression. All this is now believed to be helpful in the treatment of emotional disturbances.

CHAPTER NINE

The Quacks

IT WAS A MEMORABLE DAY for the city of Strasbourg. People who had been the pawns of wars between Germany and France and had often been ravaged by one or the other were happy to ogle a spectacle that had nothing to do with siege or occupation.

A train of heavily loaded wagons rattled through the narrow cobblestone streets. They were preceded by a carriage decorated in gold, its windows covered by black curtains. It was left to the imagination of the onlookers to picture the mysterious passengers inside. A coachman with the letter C embroidered on his brocade livery swung the whip. Foreriders preceded the caravan. Who was coming to town? Royalty? The Emperor himself? Perhaps the Pope?

The new arrival had no intention of keeping his identity a secret. At first it was whispered from person to person, and then shouted from the streets to the open windows high above where other curious watchers gaped. "It's Count Cagliostro, the great doctor. He is the one who can heal anybody."

Stories of how the count had made the lame walk and the bedridden rise and how he had provided lepers with new skin and healthy limbs and beautiful faces made the rounds of alleys and city squares.

Cagliostro and his beautiful wife Lorenza immediately rented the most luxurious house in town. A small army of servants emptied the wagons of costly carpets, furniture, and jewelry. Cooks set up shop and began to prepare exotic dishes which nobody in Strasbourg had ever tasted or heard of.

Rumors were thick about the mysterious past of the newcomers, and Cagliostro saw to it that they kept growing ever more fanciful. It was said that the Count was really several thousand years old. If he did not look it, it was just that he was well-preserved. Several of his servants let it slip out over mugs of local beer that they had been with the master's household two or three hundred years. "He possesses the famous Philospher's Stone," they told their awestruck drinking companions. "One touch of the stone will turn copper, tin, or any other ordinary metal immediately into gold. He is also the only man alive who knows how to make up the elixir of life. This draught keeps the drinker eternally young. He drinks it every morning."

The vision of never-ending youth had been dreamed for ages. In their dank and drafty laboratories, medieval alchemists had mixed and boiled mysterious combinations of liquids. They had hoped that some mixture would succeed in keeping away the specter of old age and death. Arnold de Villanova, a thirteenth-century alchemist, used brandy distilled from wine as one of the ingredients for his experiments. When he found that the brew not only tasted very good, but also made him feel happy and vigorous—at least for a while—he named the supposed youth-preserving medicine *aqua vitae* (water of life).

Some types of strong hard liquor are still called aquavit today. Arnold and other alchemists worked under the assumption that they might be able to extract the "life spirit" from grapes and other fruits. Today we still refer to strong alcoholic drinks as "spirits."

What the medieval alchemists tried vainly to accomplish, Cagliostro boasted to have successfully perfected.

It was also rumored that Cagliostro regularly talked with the spirits of persons long dead, people with whom he had associated in previous centuries.

The Cagliostros worked hard at making themselves liked in their new surroundings. They entertained the leading townspeople lavishly. Every day the Count made himself available to the sick of the city. Only the most courageous people came at first. But soon they appeared in huge numbers, coming not only from Strasbourg, but also from far away. Sometimes the Count "treated" five hundred individuals a day. Those who could, paid him; the poor were not charged a single copper.

The treatment was always the same; it made no difference if the patient was bleeding, feverish, or chilled. The Count drew with his forefinger some mysterious lines over the forehead of the afflicted. The signs were supposed to have been imparted to him, centuries ago, by famous magi in the Middle East. Then he placed on the patient's lips a single drop of the celebrated elixir of life. Uttering strange words and tracing grandiose figures in the air with his hands, the healer finally retreated behind rustling velvet curtains shrouded in a fog of Oriental incense.

By then the visitor was so utterly dumbfounded by the proceedings and the splendid setting that he almost forgot why he had come in the first place. He left, convinced that his health had miraculously improved. The Count's fortunes prospered. Noble ladies, wealthy merchants, and high church dignitaries sought him out. The presents they gratefully sent to the rented mansion allowed Cagliostro to hire still more servants and to engage in even more startling extravagances.

Then the bubble burst. The earliest visitors to the Count, who had believed themselves completely restored to health, saw the old symptoms of sickness reappear. Bald men who had paid fortunes for a new growth of hair found their heads as shiny as before. Several supposedly cured clients died soon after the "treatment." A few remedies dispensed by the Count even turned out to be poisonous.

When things became too uncomfortable in Strasbourg, the Cagliostros moved on to Paris where, for a while, they were even more successful. The couple became the rage of high society and were received in the most exclusive salons.

The Count added some new twists to his medical activities. He sold chairs which were said to free from rheumatism anyone who sat on them. Other merchandise successfully marketed included a powder guaranteed to make the ugliest person instantly beautiful. There was no scarcity of influential and well-educated people who believed in Cagliostro. Painters vied with each other to do his portrait and sculptors his bust.

But the day came when the air of Paris also became too sticky for the Cagliostros. They wandered on. It was soon discovered that the famed count was in reality a completely unschooled fellow by the name of Joseph Balsamo. He grew up in Palermo on the island of Sicily without any title of nobility. As a young man he was run out of town for cheating several jewelers, and that was the beginning of Cagliostro's shady career. In 1795 that career came to a sad, though not entirely undeserved end in the dungeons of a Roman prison.

So ardent is the quest for health and long life that people lose all sense of judgment when these things are promised. This is still true today, to some extent, and was certainly a fact in the eighteenth century.

The grossest swindle, the most obvious scheme of deception found believers. They paid the price, impressed by the showmanship and enticing promises of the quack. There were those rogues who, like Cagliostro, rode in fancy carriages and received their victims in marble palaces. Others, less fortunate, drove rough-hewn carts from village to village and plied their trade at fairs and on market days. Like any other huckster, they barked out their cures and remedies until a sizable crowd had assembled. Then a helper who played the part of an ailing onlooker came forward for treatment. Soon he threw away his crutches or straightened out his arched back, shouting, "I am cured . . . I can walk again . . . The pain is gone."

The roving quacks sold cramp rings and liver pills. They offered false topaz stones to be used against blindness and "celestial beds" on which women would be sure to bear lots of healthy children. Various colored liquids were said to be effective against different diseases. Snake oil was advertised as a multipurpose medicine even though the Bible designates the serpent as an ally of evil.

An item which served many generations of quacks as a very lucrative piece of merchandise was the widely praised Bezoar stone. Actually it was not a stone at all, but a brown clot that had been formed in the intestines of animals, mostly goats, much as gall stones form in the human body. The possessor of a Bezoar stone believed that it would protect him from poison. Even after poison was swallowed, the stone would serve as an antidote. No wonder that Bezoar stones were popular with politicians and, at times, even with royalty. They were constantly afraid of rivals who might put something too strong into their wine or soup.

Some fake healers combined their main trade with sideshows. To attract customers, they brought along musicians, singers, and comedians. If nothing else, the customer at least enjoyed some entertainment for his money. While being treated for stomach cramps or weakness of the kidneys, one could also have a few teeth pulled by the same operator. He even removed cataracts, often with disastrous effects.

All this is not to say that quacks were never successful. Many people who came to these "healers" went away feeling fine, thoroughly persuaded that what was troubling them had been cured. Nor were all the ointments, salves, and powders sold on the market square useless or dangerous. Many an unschooled huckster of nostrums had nevertheless picked up a lot of popular knowledge about herbs and barks with healing effects. A good example is fox glove, a flower with fingerlike blooms. It was often prescribed by itinerant healers and also used in magic healing rites. Much later in history, it was discovered that the plant was anything but useless. It is the raw material for *digitalis* (digit means finger in Latin), a widely used medicine for combating heart disease.

The quack specialized in instant diagnosis, followed by immediate cure. This all had to be accomplished in one quick encounter. Otherwise—no sale. Around 1910 a German sheep herder turned doctor diagnosed all forms of sickness immediately by pulling three hairs from the neck of the patient and holding them against the light. Other quacks came to instantaneous conclusions by looking for a moment at a vial filled with urine. Before the sick person could count to three, the verdict was pronounced: "Your stomach is full of pimples." "There is a lot of dust in your lungs." "A ball of hair is blocking your bowels." The treatment followed without any waiting period.

One ingenious practitioner hailing from Berlin treated all aches and pains by putting a chunk of white cheese on the afflicted part of the body. If it did not help, it was at least harmless.

The rise of modern technology brought great general interest in all sorts of machinery, in engines, and in electricity. Quacks soon learned to put the new developments to their own use. They invented various gadgets that flashed or turned or made strange noises and acclaimed them as universal tools for diagnosis and treatment.

An unschooled peasant from Upper Austria, Valentin

Zeileis, designed a glass tube equipped with electrodes which could give out sparks and a fluorescent light. It also made crackling sounds. The machine was something that could be duplicated in any high school physics laboratory. With that formidable instrument, Zeileis stroked the bodies of quivering patients. With only a couple of strokes of the flashing glass tube, he knew what the problem was. "It's your liver," he diagnosed, or, "Buddy, your left lung is all worn out." He had a list of twelve diagnoses handy, and without showing the slightest hesitation he made his choice from this dozen. As treatment, the wonder healer administered a few more strokes with his gadget, and his visitors went away joyous.

Zeileis, now a millionaire, bought an old castle. The courtyard was always crowded with patients who waited there for hours in any kind of weather. At the entrance to the main buildings stood the famed healer in shirtsleeves and chewing a fat cigar. As the clients passed by in single file, he collected the tickets which had to be purchased in advance, as if they were for a circus performance. The next stop for the patients was a darkened room where everybody had to strip to the waist. There was no pretense of privacy. When a whole batch of patients was assembled, Zeileis appeared with his tube ready for action. It took him only a minute or two per individual.

Despite the humiliating treatment, the people kept coming, several thousand a day, simple laborers and their wives, as well as the educated citizens of Vienna. Those whose health improved after one or several visits to Zeileis trumpeted his wonder-working far and wide. The others who continued to suffer remained silent, ashamed that they had been duped into throwing away good money.

Zeileis' practice grew to such proportions that he trained his sons to assist him. One of them even obtained a regular medical degree from the University of Vienna, not because it was needed to do the job, but in order to circumvent Austrian laws against quackery.

The quack practiced his trade on all continents; he still does. It has never been possible to draw a sharp line between the quack and the more scientifically inclined practitioner of medicine. Girolamo Cardano was a pioneer of medical science in sixteenth-century Italy. But while he occupied himself with mathematical and biological studies, he also believed in demons and various occult powers. Many of his speculations centered on the mystical connection between man's health and numbers, such as the date of birth. Whatever his knowledge or lack of it, Cardano made one observation which shows common sense and has not lost any of its validity to this day: "A physician is successful when the patient believes in him."

North America proved to be an ideal field of activity for the inventive quack. It was, until not so long ago, a vast expanse of nearly empty land where trained physicians were scarce and rural populations had very little contact with the outside world. Life was full of hardships. Accidents and illness loomed as ever-present threats.

Some American quacks were actually doctors gone wrong. They had studied medicine, as much as there was to be studied at that time, but had decided that they could make more money with some nonmedical gimmick which they proclaimed could heal everything immediately. One such medical doctor who did not stick with his training was Elisha Perkins. Dr. Perkins had practiced regular medicine for years in Connecticut. But one day, around the middle of the eighteenth century, he presented Perkins' Patent Tractors to the startled world. The contraption consisted of two rods about three inches long, rounded on one end and pointed on the other. One rod was brass, the other iron, and they were to convey magnetic impulses into sick bodies.

Dr. Perkins lectured that all one had to do was draw the "tractor" slowly over the aching part of the body, always from the center toward the periphery. To do it in the opposite direction would make the condition worse instead of better. "If there is no immediate effect," he advised, "press down on the body and repeat."

The doctor constructed the devices in his own home and sold them at a profit of several hundred percent. Much more money poured in than he could have made from a standard medical practice.

In order to sell his tractors, Perkins traveled all over the American colonies. What did it matter that he was expelled from the Connecticut Medical Society when such cities as Philadelphia received him with open arms. Even George Washington bought a set of tractors, and another gentleman farmer from Virginia sold his plantation to invest the whole proceeds in Perkins' devices.

But in England, the doctor had tough luck. A Dr. Haggarth at Bath painted some wooden sticks to resemble metal ones. His patients, believing the sticks to be tractors that gave out magnetic impulses, immediately claimed to be cured of gout, rheumatism, and other troubles. Perkins was laughed out of England. In 1799 he fell victim to an epidemic of yellow fever which swept the eastern seaboard, unable to save himself with his own gadget.

Perkins was outdone by Dr. Hercules Sanche, who put not just one, but two healing contraptions on the market and even had them patented. He began his practice late in the nineteenth century. Even at that date, a doctor's title was not always proof that a serious medical education had been obtained. A number of so-called medical schools were mere degree mills.

Sanche's first invention was the "electropoise," a small

metal cylinder with an elastic cord on one end to be fastened to the wrist or ankle. Then came the improved model, the "oxydonor," which sold for $35. The advertisement stated very definitely that it "cures all forms of disease. It cures all fevers, including yellow fever, in a few hours."

All the afflicted person had to do was place the oxydonor, also cylindric in shape, into a bowl of water. The cylinder contained nothing but a stick of carbon. With the help of a small disk the whole contrivance was attached to the ankle of the patient. The patient was told: "Just relax while your body absorbs the oxygen, and you will be well in no time." A display ad in the newspapers featured a pretty woman reclining on a couch with an oxydonor attached to her shapely leg. That helped, of course, to boost the sales figures tremendously. Eventually, the post office and other public agencies began to make things uncomfortable for the inventive Dr. Sanche, but he evaded them by moving from place to place, and eventually crossing the border into Canada.

There was—and still is—no end to the phony cures and patent medicines peddled both to the ignorant and to those who should know better. These people are either taken in by fraudulent promotion or are so desperate that they are willing to try anything.

Cure-all foods have been sold which were nothing but doctored-up cottage cheese. In several instances, clever promoters brought out potions which contained as their main ingredient a good measure of alcohol. Sometimes a laxative was mixed in with it, like in the "Black Draught" that was sold in the South following the Civil War. Naturally, everybody who drank such stuff felt good—for a time. But whatever ailed the patient was still there after the effect of the "medicine" had worn off.

It is not always easy to distinguish between the faith healer and the quack. The difference lies in the intention of the healer. Does he work out of a religious conviction or does he knowingly commit a fraud to line his pockets? Some operatives claim to act under divine inspiration, but most observers class them as phonies and cheats. Even so, they retain a faithful following, people who stoutly maintain that they have been helped. An example of this is the case of the so-called psychic surgeons in the Philippines.

Tony Agpaoa has been practicing in Manila for many years and has seen thousands of patients. They have come all the way from the United States and Europe. Tourist agencies organized special package tours that included airfare, hotel accommodations, and treatment by Tony. Every week a new plane load was flown in until the Federal Trade Commission stepped in. But ailing people kept on coming, attracted by the hard-sell promotion which featured filmed testimonials from supposedly cured cancer and multiple sclerosis patients. Several far-out small churches aligned themselves with the psychic surgeons.

"Dr." Tony was not always a healer. He dropped out of school early, and in Detroit he jumped bail when indicted for fraud. But in the Philippines he found his true calling.

Every morning dozens of people crowd into a hotel room which serves simultaneously as waiting room, office, and operating hall. The next patient in line is called forward by Agpaoa, who stands there clad in a sports shirt. The patient lies down on a cot, and the healer immediately diagnoses cancer of the stomach. With his bare hands, he performs an operation lasting fifteen to twenty minutes. He mutters something that could be a prayer and then presses his hands against the patient's abdomen. Soon a red, blood-like substance spreads on the exposed skin. Then Agpaoa raises one hand, in which he holds a piece of fatty tissue. "Here is the tumor," he proclaims. "It's all out now." The affected part of the body shows no trace of a wound or a scar. This is "psychic surgery."

To vary the procedure Tony sometimes sucks the painful area by mouth and then comes up with a piece of bone between his lips. He shows it around triumphantly. "Here, this is what was hurting you. Now it is out. No more trouble." He has just performed an age-old witch doctor's trick.

Professional magicians who make their living doing sleight-of-hand manipulations maintain that they can duplicate any of Dr. Tony's operations with the help of some animal tissue and red ink.

Courts have prevented "psychic healers" from operating within the United States. Before the ban, a reporter claiming to be in need of a cure visited a psychic healer in Oregon and later testified at a court hearing. "The whole business is extortion of thousands of dollars from hundreds of poor, sick, and gullible people," she said.

Still, the psychic surgeons have their defenders: critically ill people who have made the rounds of legitimate physicians to no avail and also seekers of mystic experiences who close their eyes to factual evidence. Agpaoa insists that he is only the instrument of a higher power. He says: "I do not know what I did, what I cured. God heals through the healer. Unknown forces command my fingers."

Another successful healer, financially successful, that is, is Norbu Chen. This man surrounds himself with religious symbols of the Far East. A statue of Buddha dominates the dimly lit treatment room of this ex-convict from Houston, Texas. Incense burns in brass braziers. Recorded chants and the sound of a gong are heard as the healer enters clad in a black robe with a strangely ornamented necklace around his neck. The diagnosis is given in a flash. "You have a prostate problem," Chen declares with finality. The healing itself consists of a form of massage. As he explains it: "I press on certain parts of the body and I transmit energy to those points." The visitors gladly leave a voluntary offering before they exit.

These ill people had come deeply upset, with their rational defenses down, unable to make reasonable judgments. They departed, desperately wanting to believe that they were now better off.

~~~~~~

CHAPTER TEN

Mesmer, the Magnetizer

EIGHTEENTH-CENTURY VIENNA was a delightful place to live for those who had money or high office or both. In the cavernous imperial palace with its baroque archways and domes, the Empress Maria Theresa ruled over the steadily growing Austrian empire. Her daughter, Marie Antoinette, had married the King of France, not out of love, but to cement the new alliance between the two countries.

In the beautiful capital shaded by the green Vienna woods, the many poor people could barely keep from starving. But for the upper echelons life was good. Among the many pleasures offered was the enjoyment of superb music.

To this privileged minority belonged Franz Anton Mesmer, a respected physician who had had the good sense to marry a wealthy widow. He owned a spacious home just off the tree-lined boulevards that ringed the inner city. Whatever time he could salvage from his medical practice he devoted to music. For a layman he could perform well on the piano and cello. He had also invented a new musical instrument, the glass piano, which consisted of a set of glass bowls mounted on a rotating spindle. By drawing wet fingers across the rims of the bowls one could produce sounds of different pitch, and so play a tune.

Mesmer liked to organize musical evenings in his salon, a large living room with crystal chandeliers and brocade tapestries. Some of Vienna's most renowned musicians were welcome guests there. Wolfgang Amadeus Mozart often came to play and to listen.

Dr. Mesmer inspired confidence in his patients. He appeared to be competent, yet not immodest. His bearing was cautious and reserved. Every indication pointed to a continued successful, but quiet career without any explosive disturbances.

But this was not to be. The façade of Mesmer's reserved behavior covered an unruly spirit, a yen for venturing into new territory and uncovering what was hidden behind convention and customary acceptance. He had played with the notion of studying theology and philosophy before deciding on medicine. Although he had a good practice, he was frustrated by the low level of medical knowledge available in his day. In too many instances, when confronted with a disease, the honest doctors could only shake their heads and admit their helplessness, while those not so honest resorted to quackery.

Even as a medical student, young Mesmer could not refrain from speculating about the mysteries of existence beyond our earth. His doctoral thesis had the title, "About the Influence of the Planets," and pursued the very old ideas that the planets influence all living creatures, including man. Mesmer's theory was that this influence occurred in the form of an invisible sort of fluid coming from the stars and pervading everything. Neither stone nor metal nor the human skin could stop the fluid, he thought. Such a theory was not entirely new. In ancient times, priest-astrologers had linked the fate of humans to the moon, the planets, and the stars.

As Mesmer pondered the mysterious connection between heavenly bodies, a connection without any physical ties, such as cables or strings, it occurred to him that there existed a similar connection between magnets and the metal objects that magnets attract or push away. Magnets have fascinated people for untold centuries, especially in connection with health. They were given or sold as health-preserving amulets in Egyptian temples and later in European monasteries.

How did magnetic attraction work? Did it have anything to do with illness and pain? These were the sorts of questions that captivated the restless, searching mind of the Viennese doctor. A theory finally took shape in Mesmer's mind which had never been taught at the University of Vienna. The all-pervading invisible life force which flows from the planets into all human bodies is the same force that activates magnets and makes them attract pieces of metal. Illness is a weakening of this invisible fluid, the life force within the body. Magnets can pump new life energy into the ailing organism and make it strong again. Mesmer came forward with the claim that he had discovered a new way to treat diseases that defied the traditional ointments and draughts. It was the use of *animal magnetism*, as he called it.

This was the turning point in his life. From then on, he would cure illness by placing small magnets on the diseased spots of his patients' bodies to give the fluid of life an opportunity to assert itself. Even the shape of the magnet assumed special significance. Mesmer preferred heart-shaped magnets to symbolize the central importance of the human heart. When more than one part of the body needed healing, several magnets were applied at the same time. Mesmer felt greatly encouraged early in his new career when a woman came to him complaining of several aches. They went away quickly after he had applied three magnets.

As the news of the wonder cures spread through the city, Mesmer was swamped with people seeking relief from all sorts of ailments that were beyond the current skills of his colleagues. Inquiries and urgent invitations also came from other parts of the Austrian monarchy. It did not take long until mail began to arrive from Munich, Hamburg, and even farther away.

Mesmer's most famous case, one which brought him first honors and later trouble, was his treatment of Fräulein Maria Theresia Paradies. This young lady suffered from a supposedly incurable eye weakness. In fact, since the age of four, she had been blind, for all practical purposes. She was frequently in severe pain and at times her whole body shook with convulsions. At such moments her eyes bulged as if they were about to pop out of their sockets. She felt completely miserable and expressed the wish to die.

This same Fräulein Paradies was known in Viennese musical circles as an accomplished pianist. She appeared in concerts with great success. A recital before the imperial court was arranged. Her namesake, the Empress, was so impressed that she granted the girl's parents a yearly stipend of two hundred gold ducats to pay for the continuation of her musical studies.

It was at this point in Fräulein Paradies' life that Dr. Mesmer came to her attention. Many doctors had been consulted about her problems. None knew how to deal with them. But when she was brought to Franz Anton Mesmer's clinic, he proceeded with great determination to cure her. He seemed to have complete confidence in his method. In session after session, he placed his little magnets on her eyes. The visits were pleasant experiences without any strain or tension. The girl looked forward to the treatments. She could hardly wait for the meetings with the tall doctor whose soothing manners and soft cool hands seemed to make her feel better even before the magnets touched her. She could see better now and even read her sheet music as she practiced on the piano. The convulsions disappeared completely.

The doctor charged no fee. He invited her to stay in his

house so that he could supervise the treatment better and dispense it more frequently. Apparently, he liked to have female patients as his houseguests. Two such ladies preceded Fräulein Paradies in that role.

Everything pointed in the direction of a major success story. Then something unforeseen happened. Rumors had been whispered for some time that the doctor had more than a medical interest in his young patient. Her parents started clamoring loudly for the return of their daughter to the family home. Perhaps they feared they'd lose the profitable imperial stipend if she no longer lived with them. Their cries sounded genuine, however, and roused widespread sympathy. As if this was not enough harassment for Mesmer, his learned colleagues now broke into a loud chorus of condemnation. Some had voiced their doubts of the magnetic cures from the beginning. Suddenly, the whole medical profession, led by Baron von Störk, the eminent personal physician to the Empress, was after Mesmer. Even the police voiced an interest in what went on in the Mesmer household.

This was too much pressure all at once. The doctor's resistance caved in quickly. Fräulein Paradies was sent home in a hurry against her own tearful protestations. Her old symptoms returned. All through the remaining years of her life, she continued to suffer from poor health. Vienna's doctors were not surprised. They had maintained all along that her condition had never really improved and that the magnetic cures had been sheer humbug. Mesmer proclaimed just as loudly and vehemently that she had made astounding progress under his care and would have been completely cured had he been allowed to continue. This was, of course, hard to disprove.

Mesmer's position in Vienna had become so unpleasant, personally as well as professionally, that he decided to go into exile. In 1778, he left behind his comfortable home, his musical instruments, including the glass harmonica, and the whole pleasure-laden atmosphere of Viennese upper-class life.

Mesmer went to Paris, the destination of so many exiles. A few short years later, a revolution would shake French society down to its deepest foundations. But, for the moment, Paris was still a major center of elegant life, the cultural capital of the western world. The court of King Louis XVI and his Austrian queen overshadowed that of Marie Antoinette's pious mother. The days of abundance and extravagant luxury seemed destined to go on forever. Nobility and wealthy merchants tried to rival the costly pleasures of royalty.

Mesmer soon consoled himself over the rough treatment he had received in Vienna. He found Paris an ideal place of operation. What had looked like misfortune turned out to be his golden opportunity. His new home offered much in the way of possibilities for a wide range of activity. Soon he had gained the confidence of the Count d'Artois, one of the foremost noblemen. This was Mesmer's entrance ticket to the highest circles of Paris society.

His practice bloomed as it never had before. He insisted now with complete self-assurance that the life-giving magnetic energy could cure all diseases no matter what organ or part of the body was affected. His next innovation was to dispense with actual magnets. That is, the magnets were not used anymore in the *presence* of the patient. Instead, Mesmer proceeded to "magnetize" water, by immersing magnets in bowls filled with water. When his client either drank the water, bathed in it, or otherwise came into contact with it, the illness would just drop off and be immediately replaced by robust health.

Mesmer was now ready to turn his system into a large-scale enterprise. He rented a spacious townhouse on Place Vendôme in an elegant section of Paris and furnished it in grand style. Like so many other healers, he considered it of the greatest importance to work in sufficiently impressive surroundings.

The most conspicuous piece of equipment in his new clinic was a large oaken tub. Two rows of bottles filled with "magnetized" water were placed in the tub. Steel rods were inserted in the bottles through pierced lids. The patient grasped the free end of the rod. In this way the invisible magnetic fluid was transmitted into his fingers and on into all parts of his body. As Mesmer's popularity and the demand for his services grew, he refined his method into a kind of assembly-line service. A large group was assembled around the tub, which he named a *baquet*. The patients linked hands. The life force could then flow from one person to the next through the room while only one or two people touched the rods.

To heighten the effect, Mesmer turned the healing sessions into very dramatic shows. Since these gatherings were patronized mostly by women, handsome young male attendants were added to the staff. As the patients waited for the appearance of the doctor, the attendants gently massaged their necks and backs. Even the waiting time became a pleasant, relaxing experience. Heavy tapestries muted shrill sounds that might have entered the spacious hall. The outside light was filtered and softened through stained glass windows. The inevitable incense burned in handsomely crafted copper containers. Even a new glass harmonica had been constructed to replace the one left behind in Vienna. An attendant produced pleasant tunes on it that lulled everybody into a light, warm drowsiness. They did not mind the prolonged idleness, seated as they were around several baquets. One such contraption could not have accommodated all who came.

A jolt went through the circles of women. In an instant they were all wide awake, fairly quivering with excitement. The great doctor himself made his entrance. He cut an imposing figure with his high forehead and his pointed beard under full lips. Light clear eyes projected an air of both power and gentleness. His costume was carefully chosen. Over a shirt of frilly lace, he wore a flowing lilac robe decorated with mystic symbols. From a gold chain around his neck dangled a magnet. Though he did not rub the skin of his patients with it anymore, the magnet still symbolized the essence of his healing system. In his hand Mesmer carried a staff of polished white ivory, the eighteenth-century equivalent of the ancient witch doctor's wand.

As Mesmer approached the nearest circle of patients, a woman became extremely agitated. She screamed wildly and her body shook uncontrollably. The disturbance spread through the whole circle and from there to the next baquet until the hall was filled with shrieking, twisting bodies. As if shot through by a real electric current, the whole assemblage alternately groaned and laughed hysterically. Some people broke into a frantic dance, sweating heavily all the while.

But as Dr. Mesmer moved with unperturbed dignity from baquet to baquet, the patients quieted down. They were utterly exhausted. There was silence, interrupted only by the hard breathing of overexertion. A few minutes later, everybody was up and alert, smiling contentedly and exchanging cheerful banter. They all gave the impression that something very pleasant had just happened to them, something that had changed the course of their lives for the better. They were convinced that it was due to the impact of the great doctor, and they expressed their thanks profusely. Some fell to their knees at his feet and kissed his hands in gratitude. To leave a generous contribution in the appropriate receptacle before leaving was the least they could do in return for such a magnificent experience.

It became fashionable among the highest social circles of Paris to meet at Dr. Mesmer's establishment. It was like going to a party and getting therapy at the same time. Dukes and duchesses hastened to reserve space at the baquets days ahead of time. Women from the French upper crust virtually threw themselves at the Austrian doctor without any effort to conceal their infatuation.

Let it be said to Mesmer's credit that he was not content to be only a society doctor, even though his coffers were filled with the fees and gifts of the rich. He never withheld his services from the less fortunate Parisians who were in the overwhelming majority. To accommodate the huge throngs who followed him through the streets and cornered him wherever he went, he decided to "magnetize" the trees on the broad boulevards and in the many beautiful public gardens. Cables were attached to the tree trunks, and everybody who held on to a cable could receive the benefits of the magnetic fluid. The numbers of simple Parisians who believed themselves healed in that way were astronomical.

From the moment Dr. Mesmer burst into the medical limelight, he was a controversial figure. The controversy still goes on. On the one hand, students of the history of healing call him just another common quack. But others are not so quick with their condemnation. Was he really staging just a clever game of deception to collect more money? He had obtained the best medical training available in his day, and he could have made a comfortable living without incurring the wrath of his professional colleagues. There are those among his biographers who give him credit for a more original feat. They feel that he stumbled on an extraordinary discovery which he himself did not fully understand. Only scholars and practitioners who came after him managed to put together the pieces of the puzzle.

Did Mesmer, a sophisticated intellectual, personally believe in his magnetized bottles and tree trunks, or was this merely a clever device to get the patients ready to accept the treatment that really helped them? It must have slowly dawned on him that whatever healing took place was due to the direct impact of his personality on the patients, rather than to unseen magnetic fluids. Without doubt, he recognized that his method was most effective when people were assembled in large groups and when the treatment came as part of an impressive, well-staged performance. Knowingly or not, Mesmer was a pioneer of a procedure that was later to be named hypnosis. Even though he pretended to pump life energy into the human body, it was, in reality, the human mind that he impressed. Therefore, he occupies a place of some importance in the development of *psychiatry*.

Mesmer had definitely come to the conclusion that it was not a piece of iron, the magnet, that did the healing, but the magnetizer. However, for very practical reasons, he kept to himself this new awareness that it was his own dramatized personal influence—the steady glance of his eyes and the touch of his elegant soft hands—that brought about the most profound changes in the patient. Yet it could not be that a doctor's eyes or fingers could make diseased organs well. Mesmer had absorbed too much medical knowledge to accept that. He never found a clear scientific explanation, but his thoughts returned again and again to the puzzle of why many signs of discomfort in his patients disappeared simply because he *suggested* that they disappear. This was at the bottom of the whole performance with magnets and baquets.

Mesmer created in his patients the will to health. That was the decisive factor. He had become convinced that he could do it just as well without all the pomp and ceremony, the soft music, the bottles, and the metal rods. But his practical knowledge of the human mind told him that people were attracted by the hidden and the obscure and the theatrical, so he continued to speak grandly of animal magnetism and of the life fluid that flows from the planets through metal and healing hands into the ailing body.

How he really felt about the whole healing process is expressed in such statements of his as: "Of all the bodies in nature, none is so potent in its influence upon man as is the body of man himself."

Be that as it may, the doctor with the bearing of a high priest took Paris by storm. Sufferers from real or imagined illnesses came from all over France and from countries beyond. They went away rejoicing in their cure from gout, paralysis of limbs, and various other evils. One reason that the percentage of Mesmer's successes was large was the careful selection of those who were admitted to the treatment. All patients with open sores were excluded, as were the mentally retarded and the obviously insane. Mesmer knew, or perhaps guessed correctly, that there was nothing he could do at that time for cases which modern psychiatrists would classify as *psychoses*.

His continuous good fortune seemed assured. A lady-in-waiting to Queen Marie Antoinette declared herself cured by Mesmer. That brought the Austrian to the direct attention of the royal couple. He had been practicing in Paris for two years when the king offered him a generous annual income on the condition that he train three Frenchmen in his methods. The doctor refused; there was no room for more than one Mesmer in France.

Because of Mesmer's refusal, the royal government withdrew its support. Louis XVI probably had nothing personally to do with this. He was a simple fellow who preferred tinkering in his silversmith's shop to affairs of state. But his advisers felt that the immigrant physician was getting too arrogant.

Nursing a grudge, Mesmer left the country. What followed

was exactly what he had hoped for. There was an outcry of dismay among friends and former patients. Since the government refused to subsidize the famous doctor on his terms, many private citizens who had benefited from Mesmer's treatments started a subscription. In twelve months they raised the astounding sum of 340,000 French livres.

Mesmer staged a triumphal reentry into Paris like a hero returning from his conquests. The jubilation of his fans knew no end. The "mesmeromania," as his critics called it, rose to astronomic proportions. At the height of his fame, Mesmer's activities were carried on in two elegant town mansions. In each one three sets of baquets were in operation at the same time. Before the street entrances, large numbers of gilded coaches could be seen lined up all day. In the bistros of the neighborhood, the coachmen waited and told exaggerated tales of the wonder doctor's prowess.

But with the growing public esteem also came a growing number of attacks by determined enemies. Sensational stories made the rounds about lurid goings-on during the magnetizing sessions. The topic was belabored in newspaper cartoons and even on the stages of Paris theaters until it became a major scandal.

Just as they had earlier in Vienna, his medical colleagues arraigned themselves solidly against Mesmer. Since the weak king did not know how to handle the situation, he appointed an investigative commission to look into the matter. Benjamin Franklin, then the ambassador of the newly independent American colonies, belonged to this commission of eminent scientists. No evidence of real healing was found. The commissioners attributed Mesmer's success to his personal impact on the imagination of the patients.

For a while the public enjoyed the give and take of outraged accusations and spirited defenses. But the whole squabble sank into immediate oblivion, swept away by the political storm that broke in 1789. French society was shaken up from top to bottom by the great revolution. Dormant forces of anger and frustration were released. Violence and terror engulfed the cities and the countryside.

The baquets stood unattended and forgotten. Many of Mesmer's noble clients were thrown into prison. Every day some of them made the trip, not in fancy carriages, but in rough wooden carts, to be publicly beheaded by the guillotine.

The prophet of animal magnetism found the situation too risky. For the second time in his adventurous career, he fled into exile. He tried in vain to settle once more in Vienna. The medical circles there made it known in no uncertain terms that he was still unwelcome. In addition, coming from the seat of rebellion against monarch and aristocracy, he aroused the attention of the Austrian police. It was not the right climate in which to start over once more. The last years of Mesmer's life were spent in a small town on the bank of Lake Constance, which nestles in a valley on the borders of Austria, Germany, and Switzerland. There he practiced his new method of medicine quietly without any outside interference.

Mesmer died in 1815, at the age of eighty-two. The world had by then largely forgotten Franz Anton Mesmer as an individual. In the meantime, animal magnetism had become very popular and was practiced by many healers on both sides of the Atlantic Ocean. And the dictionaries had a new entry, the verb *mesmerize*. It means to spellbind, to exert an especially strong influence upon a person by facing him directly.

~~~~~~

CHAPTER ELEVEN

Hypnosis Becomes Respectable

A BURLY TRUCK DRIVER slides into the dentist's chair.

Out on the highway, the man is king. He fears no one. With supreme confidence, he can ease his giant trailer rig into the tightest place. Nobody dares contest his right of way.

But now he is pale and tense. The muscles in his face grow rigid. His big hands are shaking with fear of the gleaming steel tools on the little round table.

In a quiet, monotonous voice, the white-coated doctor begins to talk.

"Just look at the little light above the table. Keep on looking. Just make yourself comfortable. Relax. Your eyes are feeling more and more tired. Your eyelids are heavy. You can't keep your eyes open. Your body is now completely relaxed. In a few seconds I am going to say 'now.' When I say the word 'now,' every muscle in your body will relax. . . . *Now.* Let all the tension go out of your body. Let your body get completely and utterly limp."

Drowsiness overcomes the man in the chair. The dentist's voice penetrates the haze. "Now I am going to take out your tooth, and you will feel no pain, no pain at all."

The operation proceeds. Dentist and assistant work without haste. There is silence except for a few words they exchange in low, unruffled voices. Absolute peace is expressed in the patient's face. His features and his completely relaxed breathing suggest deep sleep, yet his senses are alert. He hears the doctor's commands to keep his mouth open, to turn this way or that. His mind is at rest, suspended between waking and sleeping. It is in a state of *trance*.

The operation is finished. The assistant removes the apron and instruments. The dentist's voice is heard again, pleasant, soothing, like a mother's words to a little child. "I am going to wake you up. In a few seconds I will count one, two, three, and then I will tell you to open your eyes. When I say, 'Open your eyes,' you will open your eyes and feel refreshed and wonderfully relaxed and calm, better than you have felt all day. Your eyelids are no longer heavy. . . . One, two, three, open your eyes."

Obediently, the truck driver opens his eyes. He stretches his arms as if awakening from a deep, refreshing sleep. "What did you do to me this time that was different, Doc?" he asks, rubbing his eyes. "I didn't feel you give me the needle."

The big man, fearless and aggressive when enthroned in the cabin of his rig, was scared to death of visits to the dentist's office. What frightened him more than anything else was the prick of the injection needle. The prick had been missing this time. No pain-killing injection had been given; yet he remembered nothing of the actual pulling of the tooth.

This particular dentist is also a trained hypnotist. Like a number of his colleagues, he finds in hypnosis a useful tool for relieving his patients of pain. Hypnosis also helps him combat the often deep-seated dread with which many approach his office.

Modern hypnosis is a direct descendant of the impressive manipulations of people by witch doctors and priests of various sects and cults of the past. A sensational healing method very much akin to hypnosis was what made Franz Anton Mesmer famous two centuries ago. Since then there has been no letup in the public fascination with such demonstrations. Despite all the ridicule heaped on Mesmer by medical authorities and the press, he was imitated by a long string of more or less theatrical admirers.

Some rather fantastic theories were advanced to back up all the touching and massaging exhibitions. One healer insisted that the magnetic power of human hands could be increased manyfold by soaking them in vinegar. That same magnetizer also recommended stroking a glass of water one hundred times with the open hand to change its taste and make a potent medicine out of it. But it would only work with the hand held flat and the strokes executed in a wide arc, first northward and then southward.

Mesmer had been reluctant to initiate others into the secrets of his craft. To him the thought of raising a whole swarm of competitors was not a pleasing one. Yet his very success encouraged others to follow in his footsteps. Some imitators remained obscure, but others rose to fame and wealth.

Among the titled clients whom Mesmer attracted at the height of his career was one who was not content just to take the treatment at the baquet. He set out to do some mesmerizing in his own right. The Marquis Maxime de Puységur, who died in 1828, used his country estate as his laboratory and the peasant population on it as his guinea pigs. They did not mind because the landlord freed them from all sorts of aches and pains by "magnetizing" them. His cures were most successful when administered not to single subjects, but to a large number at one time. He liked to assemble the farmhands on the village green by a small brook into which willows dipped their slender branches. The willows had been duly magnetized by the marquis. All the peasants had to do was hold hands while one of them grasped a branch. The precious life fluid could then flow from right arm to body to left arm and on into the arm of the next in line.

"Just have absolute confidence in me," the landlord admonished them in a soft, yet authoritative tone. Immediately, an all-pervading feeling of contentment spread from person to person until the whole group felt transported into a sort of heaven on earth.

Victor, usually a very reserved shepherd boy in the service of the marquis, became extremely talkative when carried away by the outpouring of mass suggestion. He suddenly appeared to be reacting to a new reality which no one else could perceive. At one moment he imagined himself dancing with the most beautiful maidens in the village, although he was usually so shy and awkward that he hardly dared to look at a girl. Then he reported jubilantly that he had just won the coveted first prize at the annual shooting match, although he had never worked up enough courage to enter the contest. Victor's behavior was proof that he felt all those impossible events to really be happening. But after he was jolted out of his "trance," he had not the slightest memory of what he had said.

Going beyond Mesmer, the marquis claimed to observe that the people he had magnetized acquired abilities which they had not possessed before. They suddenly perceived what went on in places far away, and they could correctly diagnose their own illnesses. After the effects of his persuasive act had worn off, those abilities disappeared again. Puységur was the only early magnetizer who made such claims. They were to be heard again in later years.

Other mesmeric healers resembled the titled Frenchman in claiming that their most spectacular successes were with large groups assembled in one place. The Portuguese abbot José Custodia de Faria was such a claimant. The Catholic clergyman had spent many years in India and had gained some insight into the religion of Hinduism. Hindu teachings stress the vanity of material success and worldly ambitions. Man's prime virtue is to be able to look inside himself and lead a life without ties to other human beings or to goods and possessions. The model of Hindu life is the bearded, barefoot, holy man who spends his days in meditation without any regard for food, housing, or clothes. With extreme concentration on his mental being and complete disregard of his physical existence, he can slip into a state of deep trance in which he neither sees the world that surrounds him nor feels what happens to his own body. He is oblivious to heat or cold or pain. For the Westerner, the attitude of the Hindu holy man is hard to understand, but for India it is part of the human experience.

The Abbé de Faria put his Indian impressions to work in metropolitan Paris. He held daily healing sessions. Such events came to be known as *séances*, a French term still used to indicate spiritualist gatherings. The priest usually appeared before a crowd of about sixty Parisians. He selected eight to ten as the most suitable subjects for what he had in mind. He ordered them to sleep, and they promptly slipped into a state of complete repose. They remained seated, though, and even kept their eyes open. He then ordered them to stop feeling sick, and at times, it worked. The people had come feeling wretched; they left exuberant about their newfound health.

While well-known aristocrats, merchants, lawyers, and even some natural scientists succumbed to the fever of Mesmerism, the university-trained physicians continued to scoff. They branded the whole matter as nonsense and superstitious quackery, just as they had done with Mesmer. Nevertheless, here and there a learned doctor fell under the spell. He was anxious to try this form of treatment, but took care to hide his first experiments from his colleagues.

Several British physicians became curious and started to experiment. They tried the personalized Mesmerian treatment on epileptics, highly nervous patients, and children affected by Saint Vitus Dance. However, they found such terms as animal magnetism or mesmerizing objectionable. The search was on for a more suitable word.

Like Abbé de Faria, Dr. James Esdaile, a Scotsman, spent some time in India, where he was allowed to experiment on poor Hindu convicts in a penitentiary. After putting them in´o the astonishing sleep-wake condition, he performed hundreds of minor and several major surgical operations on them without using any pain-killing injections. They felt no discomfort. He attributed this to the Hindu training of disregard for the demands of the body. But when he returned to Scotland and used the same methods there in his medical practice, he got quite similar results.

A Manchester surgeon, Dr. James Braid, learned to use the technique when performing minor operations. He began by making his patients stare at the neck of a wine bottle. In time he was able to induce the sleeplike condition in no more than three minutes.

Dr. Braid was one of the practitioners who was not happy with the terms used to describe this process. "Animal magnetism" was a reminder of Mesmer's grand but unscientific speculations about fluids streaming from heavenly bodies into mortal ones. Braid searched for other words, trying out a number of possibilities and discarding them. Finally, he coined the expression *hypnotism*, after Hypnos, the ancient Greek god of sleep. The term stuck. It has remained part of our language ever since.

Yet the Manchester doctor was indignant when people began to refer to him as a hypnotist. "When you call me a hypnotist," he protested, "it suggests that I do nothing but hypnotize patients. That is not so. Hypnosis is just one of many tools I use in my profession. I also prescribe castor oil occasionally, but I am no more a hypnotist than I am a castor oil doctor."

It seems that the doctor's suggestion has been generally accepted. The word hypnotist now usually designates a person who engages in this type of activity as an end in itself. Hypnosis has become a profession in its own right. The best of its members are highly trained and know the possibilities and limitations of their skill. But this field, like so many others, has produced its share of charlatans and exploiters.

Towards the end of the last century, the general public became fascinated with the possibilities of hypnosis. It turned into a standard form of entertainment. Hypnotists traveled from place to place, performing in music halls and theaters, and at variety shows. Some hypnotists were genuine masters of the craft; others were clever swindlers who had helpers planted in the audience. A person who habitually responded quickly and easily to hypnotic suggestions was often referred to as a *medium*.

In a show, a medium could be made to hold his arm horizontally, and not even the strength of several spectators could force the arm from this position. Or the medium could be ordered to make his whole body completely rigid. Then the body was placed over the backs of two chairs which stood several feet apart. It would rest there motionless as if it were a board or a metal rod.

There were a number of performers who pretended to hypnotize themselves into complete insensitivity to pain. Even today, it sends shivers down one's spine to watch someone stretch out on a bed of sharply pointed spikes or have needles pushed through his cheeks. Staying confined inside sealed coffins is another much-applauded act. Many times all this has nothing to do with hypnosis, but depends on producing illusions. The only hypnosis that goes on is a kind of mass hypnosis of the audience by the performer.

Romantic dreamers of all kinds—poets, novelists, even philosophers—vied with the showmen in their fascination with hypnosis. There was an element of drama, of struggle and submission, in the relationship between the hypnotist and his subject.

In 1894 the French writer George du Maurier published the novel *Trilby*. Trilby is an awkward girl, thoroughly devoid of any talent, who comes under the sway of the hypnotist Svengali, a sinister, self-serving character. He discovers in Trilby an ideal medium. Under his hypnotic influence, she acquires a beautiful voice, and in time becomes a celebrated opera singer. Even at the peak of her success, she remains completely subservient to her master, who exploits her shamelessly. When Svengali dies, she immediately loses all her talent. Her brilliant career is finished. Of course, this product of du Maurier's imagination has little to do with hypnotism as it is practiced in real life.

When all fiction and illusion are cleared away and all distortion discarded, what is hypnosis all about? The truth is that we don't yet have a satisfactory explanation. We can, however, describe what it appears to be and how it works.

Hypnosis is an artificially induced state of mind and body which resembles sleep, but is different from regular sleep. In this state, the mind of the hypnotized person is under the control of the hypnotist's mind. The subject accepts uncritically whatever the hypnotist suggests and acts it out immediately.

Every practitioner has his own technique of producing this heightened suggestibility in his subject. This technique, called the *induction*, aims at complete physical and mental relaxation.

Certain words and phrases are repeated over and over in a calm, monotonous voice. The subject is shut off from any outside noise or competing impressions so that he must concentrate on his relationship with the hypnotist before him. He is asked to stare at a bright light until his eyes become tired and begin to close. All the while, his confidence in the ability and good intentions of the hypnotist is strengthened. He has no qualms about putting himself into the other person's power.

At a command, he slips into this completely relaxed drowsiness, the trance. He seems to sleep, yet is fully aware of what goes on around him. He sees and hears the hypnotist.

The hypnotist continues his monotonous speech until the original light trance deepens to the point where the whole purpose of the hypnosis can be accomplished. Now come the suggestions not to feel pain, to reveal what the patient has forgotten or refused to tell, to perform acts which he was afraid to perform before.

The suggestions of the hypnotist may carry over even after the trance has ended. He may say, "When you wake up you will not remember anything you did or said while under hypnosis," or, "After you wake up, you will no longer be afraid to ride in an elevator." The subject follows all the suggestions. No one knows exactly why.

Not everybody can be hypnotized. They are persons who dread the notion of losing control over themselves, even for a limited time. Some are afraid that they will not come out of the trance, although this never happens if the hypnotist is competent. People who strongly resent any kind of authority make poor subjects for hypnosis.

Hypnosis can accomplish many beneficial things. Complete relaxation induced by the hypnotist makes the subject forget pain. This can take the dread out of undergoing dental treatment. It can also make childbirth easier when the use of pain-killing and relaxing drugs is not advisable or is not wanted. Hypnosis can alleviate headaches, sleeplessness, and nausea. It has also been successfully applied in combating such embarrassing problems as stammering and bed-wetting.

However, the results of hypnosis are not always satisfactory. A woman in her middle thirties called on a hypnotist to cure her habit of heavy smoking. He put her into a deep trance and did what she had requested. She obeyed his suggestion after she had been awakened. But having abandoned cigarettes, she now developed an overpowering craving for food, and she soon found herself bulging with excess fat.

Blind persons can be made to see and paralyzed persons to walk provided that the trouble is in the mind and not caused by damage to the body. For example, an individual who has lost his memory might, under hypnosis, remember a very unpleasant experience which his conscious mind has suppressed. But if the memory loss is due to brain damage following a stroke or a car accident, hypnosis will not be of much use.

A hypnotist can be helpful in finding out whether or not an illness is *psychosomatic*, caused by mental disturbances rather than physical ones. Suppose a paralyzed person is put into a trance and then asked to walk. If he then walks, his problem is not organic. If the nerves or muscles that control walking are destroyed, hypnosis cannot heal them. But the process may have helped with the diagnosis of the case. The patient may still not be able to walk, but the doctor may now know more about the nature of the problem.

We all tend to forget incidents in which we did not make a favorable showing, or which were very shocking and distasteful. Yet recalling such incidents may help us overcome unreasonable fears and other difficulties. With the suggestion of the hypnotist, the covers may be removed from our memories, unless the repression has been particularly severe.

But even then, the imaginative hypnotist does not easily give up. In one case, the practitioner realized that the subject was telling lies even though he was in a trance and had been requested to tell the truth. Apparently, the truth was too painful to be expressed even in the privacy of the hypnotist's office. The subject was then asked to write down the truth. Without hesitation, the pen in his hand began to write out the true sequence of events while his mouth still continued to speak the words which covered up the truth.

The twentieth century brought the two worst manmade tragedies in history. The First and Second World Wars not only reaped an unbelievably huge harvest of human lives, but also brought damage and deprivation to untold numbers of survivors. By the tens of thousands, soldiers on the battlefields broke down emotionally. The shock of facing the hell of shells and mines and bombs caused muscle contractions and paralysis. Shell-shocked young draftees forgot who they were and what had happened to them. In this situation, hypnosis proved to be of invaluable help. It worked quicker and was less hazardous than any other possible line of treatment. Often it was the only practical treatment available. While before the wars hypnosis was not thought of as a serious tool by many physicians, it is now well-established and respected in professional circles. But it must be administered by thoroughly trained and ethical practitioners; otherwise, the results can be disastrous. The failure to bring the hypnotized person completely out of the trance could have the gravest consequences. Suppose a subject in deep trance received the suggestion that he cannot move his arms. If he is not properly "deprogrammed" after the trance ends, he may remain paralyzed for an indefinite time.

The good hypnotist will not allow such a mishap to occur. But even he will recognize that there are limits to his power. Suppose he orders his client to speak Spanish or to play the piano. Unless the subject has previously studied the language or the instrument, no hypnotist can make him comply. Hypnosis cannot replace learning and practicing.

There has been much speculation about whether an evil hypnotist can use his subjects as stand-ins for committing crimes. Stories, movies, and television plays have used such ideas, but the reality is very different. The conditioning we receive from early childhood, our whole moral training, and the models of behavior we have had before us would prevent us in almost all situations from doing under hypnosis what we would abhor doing in the waking state. A patient ordered by his hypnotist to go and murder his mother would immediately snap out of his trance. But it is conceivable, though not very likely, that big-time racketeers would employ hypnotists for criminal intentions.

There are people who believe in reincarnation. In America they number only a few, but in India millions adhere to the belief because it is an important aspect of the Hindu religion. It embodies the idea that after the death of the body the soul slips into another body. Over the centuries souls may pass through many existences. In the 1950s a fantastic story made the headlines of American newspapers. A woman claimed that under hypnosis she could remember in great detail that she had lived on this earth before, under different names and in different places. Was all this a clever invention of a publicity seeker and her interviewer or was it the real thing? The argument was never completely resolved.

Whatever the special purpose of a hypnotic session and whatever inductive technique is used, it always leads to a pleasant state of relaxation. The kind of society in which we live breeds stress and tension. To cope with their unhealthy effects, we are often admonished to relax. Much advice is given, many methods proposed about how to relax. Whatever the arguments about its other uses, hypnosis leads to ample relaxation if properly undertaken. It does not require complicated machinery. Even the hypnotist can be dispensed with, for there is such a thing as *self-hypnosis*. It can be learned from books and from hypnotist teachers.

A milder form of self-hypnosis which foregoes the deep trance is self-, or *autosuggestion*. When we practice autosuggestion, we try to persuade ourselves to act and think the right way.

A famous proponent of a simple course of autosuggestion was the French druggist Emil Coué. To a world yearning for remedies against pain, disappointment, and frustration, he proclaimed that everybody can be his own doctor. "You need the will, you need imagination, and you can accomplish anything you set out to do," he announced. Thousands were only too eager to listen to the message that they could learn to be happy and healthy.

Coué pointed out that the average person is not able to walk a narrow plank two hundred feet above the ground, but a construction worker or a roofer learns how to do it and then does it every working day. Similarly, we all can overcome the difficulties that stand in our way. Coué's process was simple; just repeat every day twenty times without fail this formula: "Day by day, in every way, I am getting better and better." Use a string of beads with twenty knots to keep a correct count.

Coué called his universal prescription, "self-mastery through autosuggestion." It was an instant success, and made Coué's name a household word. He was called to lecture and to teach his method in many countries. In the 1920s Couéism was a widespread fad. Its inventor was fawned upon as a new prophet, but he modestly declared, "I am not a miracle man. I do not heal people. I teach them to cure themselves."

The fad died down quickly, but the simple message surfaced again and again in different forms and under different sponsorships. One of the best-known advocates of a Coué-like attitude is the Reverend Norman Vincent Peale. His book, *The Power of Positive Thinking*, first published in 1952, has sold over two million copies. The Reverend Peale reinforced his message with several other books on the same theme. Most recently he published *Positive Thinking for a Time Like This*. To Coué's optimism he adds a strong religious appeal. The will to succeed supported by deep religious faith presents an unbeatable force. This combination guarantees top achievements in business, professional, or personal relations. It leads to well-balanced minds and healthy bodies. "You can win," is the key phrase.

Peale's books contain many testimonials by correspondents who were freed from diseases which had defied medical treatment. But the author differs from many faith healers in that he recommends both medical and spiritual treatment. "I do not think we should depend on faith alone to heal a physical ailment. I believe in the combination of God and the doctor."

Today we hear many voices which encourage us to make better use of the vast resources within ourselves. Much of the mental and even the physical power in every individual remains dormant for life. It can be awakened. People must learn to trust in their worthiness, to have confidence in their abilities, which are only too often grievously underestimated.

Even without endlessly reciting Coué's formula, we can admit that autosuggestion has its place. To some extent, at least, we may try to be our own hypnotists.

~~~~~~

CHAPTER TWELVE

Healers of the Mind

IT WAS A RAINY MORNING in 1885. Protected by their umbrellas, Parisians rushed quickly toward their destinations along the dripping boulevards. Through the doors of the Salpêtrière Clinic, people entered in a steady stream, but not to have any wounds bound up. They came to watch. Soon the large amphitheater where the lectures took place was densely packed.

In row upon row, medical students sat in their white coats next to graduate doctors who were taking time out from their own practices. There was also a sprinkling of nonmedical spectators, richly gowned society ladies and gentlemen with plenty of time to waste. In low voices, they discussed the unusual event they had all come to witness. Dr. Jean Martin Charcot's lectures with demonstrations of hypnosis on patients had been described in the newspapers as sensational.

The world-renowned neurologist was not only a scholar of acknowledged depth, he also had a flair for the dramatic. As in a regular theater, the house lights dimmed. Floodlights illuminated the elevated platform as orderlies in white wheeled in the first patient. Behind them strode the chief himself. His bearing was more that of a military leader than a doctor. He held himself erect. He had the forehead of a thinker, but his well-cared-for beard, immaculate stiff white collar, and conspicuous diamond needle stuck in a silken tie were the attributes of a dandy.

It had been an important day in the history of hypnosis when the famous Dr. Charcot decided to apply it in his clinic. Hypnosis was still regarded by many learned people as nothing more than a tool of entertainers and of way-out unrecognized healers. But with Charcot's reputation on their side, the proponents of hypnosis were now forging ahead with quick strides. It was soon recognized as a legitimate instrument when handled by a respected practitioner.

Charcot was a man of strong opinions, and he was always ready to stand up and fight for them. At the time, he was embroiled in a scientific dispute with an eminent colleague, Dr. Bernheim of Nancy, a town in northeastern France. Both acknowledged the usefulness of hypnosis, but Charcot maintained that only people suffering from hysteria could be successfully hypnotized. Dr. Bernheim objected. His findings led him to believe that hypnosis could also be performed on otherwise healthy persons. Eventually, he was proven correct.

Although Charcot made hypnosis respectable, there still clung to it an aura of mystery. In the mind of the general public, the hypnotist was regarded as somewhat akin to a sorcerer. This image suited Charcot perfectly, and he knew how to exploit the feelings of awe he inspired among the observers.

The man on the stretcher was about forty-five years old. He had the calloused hands of a manual worker. The doctor explained that his patient was unable to walk, and therefore couldn't work since he was employed by a heavy construction firm. The man blamed his paralysis on a diseased hip, but Charcot did not accept that explanation. "There is nothing wrong with this man's hip," he declared in a voice that brooked no opposition. "I diagnose this as a case of hysteria."

The audience had been sitting in dead silence, but now a murmur ran through the rows. The doctor had just stepped into another hornets' nest of controversy. Up to now, it had been generally assumed that there were only hysterical women. Charcot was later proven to be correct in stating that men could suffer from hysteria also.

The sonorous voice on the platform continued: "As I said, the hip is in good condition. This means that the paralysis of the hip really originates in the man's mind. There must be some cause which he cannot or will not divulge to us. Therefore, to get to the bottom of this, I will now hypnotize him."

The poor patient was already in a state of bewilderment from the unusual surroundings in which he found himself. He had never been on a stage, he had never faced a large audience. He was already so far gone in his daze that only a few halting sentences spoken calmly and authoritatively by Charcot sufficed to put him into the expected trance.

"I maintain now that not only your hip, but also your right arm is paralyzed," intoned the doctor. Immediately, the arm dropped like a dead weight over the side of the stretcher.

"Will two colleagues please step up and examine the patient? You will find that the arm shows all the characteristics of real paralysis." Needless to say, the examination bore out what Charcot wanted to demonstrate.

"Now, ladies and gentlemen, we come to the main point. I have found that, under deep hypnosis, the patient's memory clears up to an astounding degree, as if he had suddenly become clairvoyant. He can remember things long forgotten, and we hope that in this case the newly awakened memories will include the events which brought about the hysterical symptoms."

Turning to the workman on the stretcher, he spoke in the commanding tone of an all-powerful ruler: "You will now remember what made you feel that your hip was diseased and that you could not walk. Tell me. Think back carefully. Don't hold anything back. Speak now."

The patient choked and then began to whisper. His words were barely audible beyond the first rows. His story was that there had been a real hip injury quite some time ago. It had been caused by an accident at work. But the injury had long since completely healed. During the time of his recovery, the worker had received financial help from the company which employed him. He developed an unreasonable fear of facing the moment when this help would be withdrawn. Accident insurance, as we know it, did not exist at the time. The dread of other accidents and the lack of confidence in himself had made a cripple out of a sturdy man.

The doctor's voice was heard again. "You now know what is behind your lameness. You need not be lame again. When you return to your job, you will be careful and not have any more accidents. In a few seconds I will wake you up. Then you will rise from this stretcher and walk alone off the stage."

As the patient made his exit, the audience broke into thunderous applause. They stomped on the floor with their feet and banged the desk tops in front of them.

One young physician in the audience was so impressed by what he had just witnessed that he forgot all about stomping and desk-banging. Dr. Sigmund Freud had almost become hypnotized himself by the events on the stage. He had traveled from Vienna specifically to find out what was behind the clamor about Charcot's startling discoveries.

Dr. Freud was a specialist in the treatment of nervous diseases. He met his patients in a modest walk-up office only a few blocks from the university medical school of Vienna. In the apartment which adjoined the office, he lived with his wife and six children, three sons and three daughters.

Freud was a frustrated man. He wanted to help his patients, but was dismayed when he realized that he did not know how. The professors under whom he had studied were as helpless as he was. Only they were too arrogant to admit it. Their wealthy patients expected from them some action, or at least some advice. So they sent them off to one of the popular and expensive spas like Vichy, Wiesbaden, or Karlsbad. The cures there brought no permanent help, although the guests had a good time. Soon after their return, they felt miserable again, and after a while they were off to another spa.

This was not the way Sigmund Freud practiced medicine. He wanted to get to the bottom of the enigma. Only by patient research and careful observation could he hope to break through the barrier of ignorance.

His patients were mostly upper middle-class women with obvious signs of strong emotional disturbances. He did not know what to do with them. Even for many who complained about body pains, he could find no remedy. Nothing seemed to be wrong; that is, nothing that would show up in a physical examination.

Freud had long suspected that the troubles of his patients had to do with what went on in their minds. But when he asked them about it, he could get no satisfactory answers. It was not that they lied to him or refused to tell. They actually knew no more than he did about what caused their symptoms. Yet the causes had to be there somewhere, hidden in the recesses of the mind. If only there was a way to get at them.

It was during this dilemma that he became aware of hypnosis. Perhaps this was the vehicle that could reach the innermost parts of the human mind. Nobody else in Vienna wanted to have anything to do with hypnosis. For the stuffy professors, the very word was an abomination.

This then was what drove Sigmund Freud to Paris and into

the auditorium of the Salpêtrière Clinic. Dr. Charcot's work looked like the answer to his own search. Freud wanted to know more, but how was he, a young unknown medic, to approach the famous man? He thought of an approach. He tried it and it worked. His voice trembled a little as he introduced himself to the Parisian neurologist and offered to translate his books from French into German. The offer was accepted. In the more intimate contact between translator and writer, Freud had the opportunity to learn whatever Charcot had to offer on the subject of hypnosis.

Back in Vienna, Freud joined hands with Dr. Joseph Breuer, an older colleague and close friend. They began to hypnotize patients, and what Freud had suspected turned out to be true. Under hypnosis, patients began to recall long forgotten events. Like the construction worker at the Salpêtrière, they kept on digging up happenings of the past until they hit on an occurrence that proved to be a clue to their present predicament.

One day a woman was brought into Freud's office. She had been badly crippled for years. A thorough physical examination could discover no cause for the handicap. Hypnosis seemed to be called for. In a deep trance, Fräulein Elizabeth began to recall the past. She revealed that once, long ago, she had been secretly in love with her brother-in-law. Then her sister, the love object's wife, died. Although Elizabeth had nothing to do with the cause of death, she nevertheless felt guilty. The deeply buried feeling of guilt made her punish herself. Living out her years as a cripple was the punishment, although she was not aware of it. When this chain of events became unraveled, the doctor was finally able to make the correct diagnosis. But before he could think of a remedy, the lameness in his patient had disappeared. When Fräulein Elizabeth finally grasped the real cause of her problem, it was like an act of purification. The guilt was gone.

She had experienced something akin to the remission of sins following a Catholic person's confession to a priest. Elizabeth's health was restored. There was no more need for self-punishment.

Another of Freud's patients, a middle-aged widow, came down with a severe attack of asthma every time her daughter made plans to move out of her house. Without being aware of it, the mother used these attacks to bind her daughter to her, to prevent her from leaving and establishing her own existence.

From a number of such cases, Freud developed a new method of treating emotional disorders. Being a philosopher as well as a doctor, he enlarged his thoughts until they encompassed a whole, completely original view of what the human mind was like. This transformed the humble practitioner into a highly controversial figure, as Freud was not content to keep his thoughts to himself, but began to publish them in various books.

Reactions to his ideas ranged from ridicule to horror. Many condemned him as a completely immoral person. But whatever opinions have been voiced about Freud's work, he must, without a doubt, be counted among the major influences on our modern ways and thoughts.

Sigmund Freud concluded that the roots of many emotional and also physical illnesses reach back to the years of the patient's youth, and often to his early childhood. When it can be learned why the individual needs to act in a way that is painful and damaging to himself, the patient can be cleansed of guilt. Long repressed, unpleasant feelings disappear, and the symptoms of illness vanish. The patient is healed.

On the other hand, if only the surface symptoms—the headaches, asthma attacks, or stomach pains—are treated, real and permanent healing cannot be achieved.

Freud went even farther in his dissection of the human

personality. As an engine runs on fuel, so, he maintained, an individual is propelled by powerful natural drives, particularly the sex drive, which makes certain that the species continues to reproduce.

According to Freud, the sex drive, the *libido*, is part of our existence from birth to death. It takes on various forms as we move through the different stages of life: childhood, adolescence, and adulthood. The thought of the sex drive being active even in small children brought immediate, strong objections.

Freud continued his portrayal of the human mind as having three distinct parts. There is, first, the *conscious* mind. It encompasses all thoughts of which we are aware. We *know* that we know. A student is fully aware of his feelings toward his English teacher or traveling companion. An adult knows that he enjoys bowling but dislikes comic books.

But there also exist thoughts and feelings of which we are unaware. Seemingly these thoughts have been forgotten, but, according to Freud, they still exist buried deep in the *subconscious* mind. There they lie hidden for years, often forever, because they have been pushed down, repressed, by the third factor in the human mind, our *conscience*. The conscience is the invisible censor inside us. It rejects the thoughts and the desires that go against the rules of conscious moral behavior. What rests in the subconscious primarily concerns unacceptable sexual yearnings, such as a boy's infatuation with his mother or a girl's with her father. The boy is then jealous of his own father, the girl of her mother. Freud finds that such feelings are common among most children at a certain stage of their development. This idea, which he called the *Oedipus Complex* in boys and the *Electra Complex* in girls, became the target of especially vicious attacks by Freud's adversaries.

We must remember that Freudian thought surfaced at a

time when society in general and the medical profession in particular had a very narrow-minded atitude toward anything even remotely connected with the subject of sex. Freud's difficulties were compounded by the fact that he was Jewish. Many influential academics in Vienna and elsewhere harbored strong anti-Jewish feelings.

Freud soon found out that he was not very good as a hypnotist. He also met patients who absolutely defied any attempt to hypnotize them, no matter how hard he tried. This spurred him on to seek another way to probe the human mind. He discarded hypnosis completely and developed his own method. This became known as *psychoanalysis*.

The psychoanalyst has his client lie down on a couch and relax. The patient is not put into a trance. The analyst then invites the patient to report anything that comes into his mind without holding back, no matter how silly or unimportant or embarrassing the thoughts appear to be. The patient is also asked to recall any dreams.

By this method of "free association," the analyst hopes to gradually roll back the covering layers of the conscience, or *super-ego*. The aim is to penetrate to the subconscious mind, and discover there the origin of the disturbance. If the analyst is successful, the result is similar to the one sought by other therapists through hypnosis.

The psychoanalyst can only succeed by establishing rapport with his client. He has to impress the client with his good intentions and with his fitness. This enables him to cross all the barriers which people usually set up to protect their privacy and shortcomings. In a way, the psychoanalyst is the modern cousin of the preliterate medicine man, the ancient priest, the faith healer, and the magnetizer.

In time, Freud attracted an adoring following in Europe and America. The admirers regarded him almost like a biblical patriarch; and like a modern Moses, he demanded absolute loyalty. Followers whose ideas only slightly deviated from his were sharply reprimanded. Several smaller groups broke away. Although acknowledging their debt to Freud, they struck out in different directions.

But whether they were accepted totally or partially, or completely rejected, Freud's teachings had a profound impact. They influenced not only medicine, but also literature, art, education, and even theology. The appearance of Freud on the medical horizon caused a revolution in the fields of *psychiatry* and *psychology*. Psychiatry deals with the diseases of the mind, and the nonmedical science of *psychology* studies human thought, feeling, learning, and emotion.

Before Freud, psychiatry had been a stepchild among the medical specialties. It had tried, mostly in vain, to trace mental illness to damage in the brain or nervous system. Now the psychiatrist and psychologist study the subtleties of the human mind in depth. The more secrets they discover, the more enthralled they become with the complexity of our mind.

Along with the heart specialist, the psychiatrist is the most talked and written about member of the medical community. He is often looked up to as more than a physician. People expect answers from him for all the ills of our society, and they listen to his pronouncements with reverence.

Since the 1890s when Freud's writings first appeared in print, they have been hotly debated inside and outside the profession. Some of his basic teachings found wide acceptance. Younger psychiatrists rejected some parts of the master's concepts while retaining others. Since psychoanalysis, as taught by Freud, is a lengthy and costly process, various shortcuts have been developed. The discovery of relaxant and stimulant drugs have greatly influenced and shortened the treatment of mental disorders; so have electrotherapy (treatment with electricity) and hydrotherapy (treatment with water).

But the basic instrument in the psychiatrist's toolbag is still psychotherapy, the face-to-face confrontation of mind-healer and health-seeker. Such confrontations, as we have seen, have taken place since long ago, but the healer of the past did not have a doctor's degree in medicine and a specialist's certificate in psychiatry. In psychotherapy, the mentally disturbed person is led, by persuasion, by suggestion, by gentle nudging, to understand himself and the way he acts.

Today psychotherapy is administered in many forms besides straight psychoanalysis. In *client-centered therapy*, the healer does not impose his own judgment on the patient, but lets the patient find his own solution to the problem. *Behavior modification* attempts to change a certain unsatisfactory way of behavior without deep probing into past experiences. For example, a person who is frightened to death when the need arises to fly in an airplane is led to overcome this fear, but the reason why he developed it in the first place is not necessarily considered. In *group therapy* sessions, several persons having similar difficulties talk out their problems under expert supervision. Alcoholics Anonymous groups and so-called encounter groups have developed out of the group approach in psychotherapy.

The demand for psychotherapy is growing rapidly. This demand comes not only from hospitals and clinics, but also from schools, nursing homes, social agencies, and prisons. Unfortunately, the great need for psychotherapy has encouraged money-hungry quacks to move in. These people promise to restore peace of mind in a few short sessions for a high price. They peddle happiness just as the quacks of old peddled worthless pills and salves as cure-alls.

Essentially, the psychotherapist imposes his will upon the person seeking his help, as did Mesmer and countless other predecessors. The help will be substantial and long-lasting if the therapist succeeds in instilling in the client a positive and wholesome outlook on his own life and on life in general. By teaching the person how to look inward, the therapist helps him find the strength to heal himself. Success in this process depends to a large extent on the therapist's ability to make his patient believe that he sincerely cares about him.

The element of strong suggestion was once applied by illiterate shamans draped in animal skins. The modern shaman is a duly initiated member of the medical guild with a personalized prescription pad and the symbol of Asclepius, the snake curling around the staff, on the windshield of his car.

~~~~~~

CHAPTER THIRTEEN

Latter-day Health Cults

MODERN HEALTH SCIENCE has arrived. At least once a year for the last half century, some startling medical breakthrough has been announced, from the cure of yellow fever to heart transplants. These scientific miracles are being performed in clinics and hospitals, in laboratories and pharmaceutical research institutes. They are among the reasons why we live longer, grow taller, and are, on the whole, healthier than our ancestors.

Yet the neighbor down the block refuses to rely on the services of a doctor, pharmacist, or lab technician. His ideas on how to keep healthy are different from theirs. He complains that the modern practice of medicine has become too cold and impersonal. It resembles an assembly line that rushes the patient through the treatment rooms as if he were a part of an automobile in a car factory. Other people deplore the high cost of quality care. And there are always some who say that the whole of medical science is on the wrong track.

Despite wonder drugs, x-rays, and open-heart surgery, thousands still seek out faith healers and miracle shrines. Many more people carry amulets as did their Stone Age ancestors. But now we put charms and amulets into places that the primitive shaman never dreamed of, such as hanging from the rear-view mirror of the family car.

Not only are the old paths of preserving health still followed, but fresh ones are being proposed that have no connection with the progress of medical science. A new Messiah still appears from time to time proclaiming a single overall cure for whatever bothers people. Followers quickly gather around to learn and apply the simple formula that will guarantee all-around health and well-being. Another health cult has begun. In most instances, its life span will be a short one.

There are cults which advocate with strong fervor a long overdue return to nature. With some justification, the cultists point at the artificiality that pervades our lives. People created industry, but instead of enjoying its products, they are being stifled by them. We eat synthetic foods that are artificially colored and flavored. We produce fake wood and stone from plastics. We alter the natural climate through air-conditioning. It is argued that we suffer so much from physical and emotional illness because we have removed ourselves so far from the wellsprings of nature. The call, "Back to nature!" is strong and persuasive. It was first heard in the eighteenth century when the great writer Jean Jacques Rousseau proposed a radical turning back from what he conceived to be the corrupting effects of civilization and progress.

Pastor Falke, a German clergyman, reached all the way back to the ancient and medieval teachings that everything in this world is made up of the four elements: air, light, water, and earth. This theory has long been discredited by modern chemistry, but to the German pastor it still sounded good. Give the four elements an opportunity to work on you, he counseled, and all illness will disappear.

His disciples did vigorous exercises in the open air, frequently plunged into ice-cold water, and submitted to compresses of wet mud. Falke declared that he could diagnose any ailment simply by looking a patient in the eye. For a while, he attracted a large following.

The longing for the lost embraces of unspoiled nature is the main motive of *naturopathy*. The message is: shed your clothes, leave the concrete jungle of the city, return to a simple life, and good health will be your reward, year-in, year-out. Various nudist clubs subscribe to such a line of thought. Other people, less radically inclined, just recommend going barefoot, sleeping in the open air, and taking frequent sun baths.

Cultish and even religious elements are noticeable in many movements that insist on natural diets. Some stick to vegetarian meals, others allow only foods grown without the application of synthetic fertilizers. A number of groups abstain from alcohol, tobacco, and drugs for either health or moral reasons, or both. The Mormons also include coffee and tea among the forbidden substances.

Another German, Samuel Hahnemann, born in 1755, was responsible for the appearance of *homeopathy*, a fad that was popular in the nineteenth century. Hahnemann started to practice medicine, but was a failure as a doctor, mainly because he did not believe in what he had been taught. His inclination was toward mystic speculations about the true nature of man. His career as a physician officially ended when he declared categorically that the medical treatments dispensed by his colleagues were useless.

Hahnemann began to concoct strange medicines of his own. By shaking the bottles in a special rhythm and pronouncing magic words over them, he wanted to free the secret spiritual forces within the chemicals so they could penetrate the mind and body of the patient.

Again it was a simple formula which, according to Hahnemann, contained the complete wisdom of healing. The Latin formula was *similia similibus curantur*—like is cured by like. His treatment: give the patient the pills which bring about the disease he already has. In other words, feed him a poisonous, harmful substance, but give it to him in such small doses or so thinned out that it will cure rather than kill him. The manmade sickness drives out the natural disorder. But the shaking of vials and the chanting of mystic words must not be forgotten, or the process will not work.

Hahnemann diluted his medicines so thoroughly that they lost all possible effect. But his contention was that by watering down the substances, their spiritual strength was increased. Whatever one thought about Hahnemann's theory, his prescriptions could do no damage because they consisted mainly of water with only infinitesimal additions of other materials. As in the case of so many other cults, the adherents of homeopathy could not be shaken in their conviction that Hahnemann's concoctions helped them.

The movement spread from Europe to the United States. It reached its height in 1900 when grateful followers erected a monument to Hahnemann in Washington, D.C. At that time, there were twenty-two colleges in this country which trained homeopathic practitioners. Hahnemann himself died in 1843, eighty-eight years old, famous, and widely acclaimed.

As it turned out later, his idea that "like is cured by like" was not all that farfetched. When the science of bacteriology developed and the true nature of many diseases was found, it became common practice to inoculate people with weakened disease-causing bacteria in order to prevent them from catching the disease in its dangerous form. In a way, this justifies Hahnemann's proposition that "like is cured by like."

The believers in *osteopathic* healing constituted a movement native to the United States. Osteopathy began with typical cultist features. Its creed was the usual simple formula, the cure-all for all maladies.

Osteopathy (Greek for "bone-treating") was the brain-child of Andrew T. Still, born in 1828. While the older cult of homeopathy made much of highly diluted drugs, Still put no trust in drugs at all. He maintained that the human body is the most complete drugstore imaginable. Any addition of chemicals from the outside would only disturb the balance and do more harm than good.

Osteopathy resorts to the past practice of manipulating the patient's body with the healer's hands, a practice that was dear to faith healers and witch doctors and priests. From the direct physical contact, the ailing person derives warmth and confidence. He revels in the healer's personal attention. The touch and stroke effect on the skin brings relief even though the regular physician may doubt its strictly medical value.

Andrew T. Still was a frontiersman from Virginia with little formal education. His love was not for books, but for machinery. Not content with a routine existence, he wandered about the open country and tried his hand at many jobs. Although his background was that of a farmer, it was rumored that he consorted with the spirit world. He could see what others couldn't.

Utilizing this kind of reputation, Still turned to healing the sick as an occupation. In those days the schooling of physicians was quite casual. There wasn't much to stop an enterprising young man from calling himself a doctor, especially in remote rural areas.

Still's interest in mechanics led him to the idea that the human body works like a machine. When a machine stops functioning, the mechanic reaches inside with his hands or with a tool and fixes the trouble. He tightens a bolt or adjusts a bearing. The same goes for the human machine. It contains within itself all the spare parts needed for repairs. Nothing need be added from the outside.

The central axle of the human machine is the spinal column. It is hollow. This allows the life fluid to flow through it. From the spinal column, the life fluid is distributed through the blood vessels and nerves to all parts of the body. Pain and illness result, according to Andrew T. Still, when too much pressure is exerted on blood vessels and nerves as they emerge from tiny openings between the vertebrae of the spinal column. A dislocation of one or more vertebrae causes the pressure and blocks the flow of the fluid. Whether the pain originated in the liver, the lungs, or the brain, Mr. Still put his hands to work to push the spinal column back into its proper shape. Often this kind of action, similar to a massage, brought temporary relief to the patient and high praise to the osteopathic healer.

Osteopathy has undergone many changes since Still's days. It has adopted many standard methods of modern medicine. The doctor of osteopathy is now an almost fully recognized member of the healing professions. In many states, osteopaths perform services almost identical to those carried out by doctors of medicine.

The osteopath's cousin, the *chiropractor*, is not a recognized member of the medical profession. Chiropratic medicine, also a product of American enterprise, is younger than osteopathy. It is still held in contempt by regular M.D.s, although it is also battling to upgrade its professional standing.

The original chiropractic concept is almost indistinguishable from the teachings of Andrew T. Still. In fact, critics maintain that D. D. Palmer, the founder of chiropractic healing, learned what he later proclaimed as his own findings from Still. Palmer started out as a magnetic healer of the old school. When he observed the success of Andrew T. Still, he took a course from him and then went on to upstage his teacher.

Palmer's new career began when he cured a janitor who had been deaf for fifteen years. Palmer made him stretch out on his stomach, and proceeded to manipulate his spine with great force. Soon the man got up and, as Palmer tells it, started to correctly answer all questions asked him.

Today chiropractors still follow the line that all illness originates in the spine. Dislocated bones irritate the nerves and must be adjusted by hand. Otherwise, the nerves cannot properly control the organs and muscles they are supposed to activate. Without seeing any need for further tests, the chiropractor then proceeds to go to work on the spinal column of his prone patient.

Osteopaths like to joke that chiropractic medicine is the first three weeks of the study of osteopathy.

Many persons suffering from rheumatic or arthritic pains swear by their chiropractor. There is no doubt the members of the profession perform valuable services to their patients, if they stay within the confines of their training. Recently, they have begun to make use of x-rays and other medical devices, but they are still not permitted to write out prescriptions or to treat their patients in regular hospitals.

It is not easy to understand why so many people are attracted to healing cults despite the astounding accomplishments of modern medical science. There is, of course, curiosity, the attraction of the unknown, the mysterious. Also, the cultist practitioner assures his followers that he has all the answers, whereas the medical doctor has to admit at times that nothing more can be done. This is not satisfactory to a patient who wants a system that explains all troubles with one statement and also recommends one type of treatment.

There are cults which go beyond the question of health. They involve an entire philosophy of life, something akin to a religion. Here health becomes tied up with the question of what is good and what is evil. Good health is considered a reward for following the right path.

This intertwining of philosophy and healing can be observed in practices that come out of the Far East.

In the last decade, our medical authorities again found cause to shake their wise heads in disapproval. A new healing fad had appeared and it was spreading rapidly. Actually, it was a very old practice, but only a handful of Westerners knew about it. Then, almost overnight, everybody was talking about *acupuncture*. Newspapers, magazines, and television gave a great deal of publicity to the art of driving away illness by sticking needles into human bodies.

The art of acupuncture had been practiced in China perhaps as long as five thousand years ago. It is intimately bound up with the world view that this magnificent civilization produced long before the West could come up with any comparable intellectual activity.

The sages taught that not only the human body, but the whole universe functions smoothly when there exists a balance between Yin and Yang. Yang is the positive, hot, expanding male energy. It brings action, growth, and progress, while Yin, the negative, dark, cold, female influence causes winter, rest, sleep, and needed regeneration. When Yang gains the upper hand there is violence and destruction, while a surplus of Yin causes death, decay, stagnation.

Now what has all this to do with sticking needles into people's ears or toes? The connection is obvious, at least to those familiar with ancient Chinese thinking. The scholars of the Far Eastern empire also saw a mysterious life force pulsing through all organs and vessels of the body, just like some of their Western counterparts. But in the Chinese context, this constantly flowing life energy is a compound of Yin and Yang. When the two elements complement each other perfectly, indicated by a divided and yet united circle, the body is healthy and functions harmoniously. Disease and pain are caused by an imbalance, and this is what the acupuncturist treats.

He has been taught that the life energy flows through the body in twelve channels, the *meridians*. When, let us say, the patient complains about pains in the back, the acupuncturist decides which meridian feeds that part of the body. In order to restore the Yin-Yang balance, he stimulates it at certain points along its pathway, perhaps in the leg or on the forehead. He does this by inserting three-inch-long steel needles into those places and twirling them lightly. Some practitioners also connect the needles with wires and send weak electric currents through them into the body.

Over one thousand acupuncture points are distributed over the twelve meridians. It is the acupuncturist's task to select the proper ones for the needles. The procedure might look frightening to the outsider, but it is painless, except perhaps for a tingling sensation around the pinholes in the skin.

As to the effects of acupuncture, it depends on who is being asked. It has now been pretty well established that it can relieve pain, at least for a time. In terms of modern science, there is no satisfactory explanation of why this occurs. As with so many other healing schemes, acupuncture helps when the patient has a strong desire to get well and has confidence in his healer. While he is being subjected to all the needle pricks, the patient is often overcome by a drowsiness not unlike the trance induced by the hypnotist. In such a state, the patient is very open to suggestions.

Strong suggestibility probably helps explain the claim of many acupuncturists that they have been successful in curing alcoholism, drug addiction, overeating, and even sexual inadequacy.

In our country the medical organizations are somewhat at a loss in how to deal with acupuncture. It cannot be condemned outright as quackery, even though Western physicians find it a strange practice. American-trained physicians with impeccable reputations have, on their visits to China, witnessed major surgical operations in which acupuncture was the only anesthetic used. While surgeons worked on their hearts or stomachs, the patients chatted with their visitors.

Acupuncture is not banned in the United States, but functions under a host of restrictions. In many states, the acupuncturist must pass a stiff licensing examination. Even then, he must either possess a medical doctor's degree himself or work under the supervision of a physician.

Obviously, most patients who crowd the waiting rooms of acupuncturists care little about Yin and Yang. Their only reason for being there is the hope that behind that door leading to the treatment room is a person who can help them, and can do it quickly.

CHAPTER FOURTEEN

Healing Religions

While trying to put a rug under a heavy piece of furniture I injured my shoulder. The pain kept me awake that night, and for two days I wasn't able to raise my arm to dress or undress. By continuing to claim my perfection as God's child, created in His image and likeness, I was free by the fourth day.

While picking a bouquet of flowers I felt a sharp sting in my hand, and a large bumblebee fell to the ground. As the arm began to hurt, I realized that God's ideas cannot harm one another. The pain stopped instantly, and there were no after-effects.

During my early study of Christian Science I had an unsightly goiter that disappeared. I never knew just when the healing took place, but later I noticed that my neck was normal. Warts on my hands were healed in several days after I clearly realized that in my true being as God's reflection I couldn't have warts. . . .

These reports appeared in the pages of the *Christian Science Sentinel*, a magazine that regularly publishes such letters from readers every week.

Christian Science is not a science like geography or geology. One cannot find it listed in the catalogs of most colleges or universities. It is a religion and has all the features one usually looks for in religions of the Western world: church buildings, services, hymns, Sunday school, and scriptures. But Christian Science has several unique traits which distinguish it clearly from other faiths. It was founded in 1879, which makes it one of the youngest religions in existence. While Judaism, Islam, and the main branches of Christianity originated in the Middle East and in Europe, Christian Science is an American product with headquarters in Boston. Another unusual feature is that its founder was a woman, whereas males have been the predominant prophets, apostles, and patriarchs in the other churches.

It was a dark night, and the weather was terrible. A lone woman was rushing home from an errand, braving sleet and a driving storm. The streets were icy. She fell down hard and lost consciousness. Fortunately, she was soon discovered and carried into a nearby house. Friends came and took her to her own home where she continued to lie in a semicoma. Occasionally, she would open her eyes and recognize her surroundings. But she was so weak that she soon lapsed back into numbness. Her friends finally gave up hope for her recovery and were trying to prepare for her death. But they were dumbfounded to see her up and dressed the following Sunday without any visible trace of illness or injury. The people who saw Mrs. Mary Baker Eddy on that day were sure that a miracle had occurred. For Mrs. Eddy herself, her recovery was a deeply upsetting experience. It provided the final thrust that made her step forward and proclaim the new religion of Christian Science.

The fall on the ice was only one of many strokes of hard luck in the life of Mary Baker Eddy. She was a controversial figure on whose head was heaped the weight of attacks as well as praise. It is hard to pass fair judgment on a leading religious personality. Followers tend to idealize him or her, while others are harsh, even cruel, in their faultfinding.

Mrs. Eddy has been hailed as a long-suffering saint, a genius of wisdom, an inspired prophetess, and a wizard at management. Others point out that she was emotionally unstable, that she imagined illnesses. Critical biographers have stated that she lived off the charity of other people and then mistreated them as a reward. She was accused of being domineering, of exploiting those who were devoted to her. Finally, the charge of plagiarism was raised. It was said that a good part of what she presented as her own teachings was actually rewrites of somebody else's ideas. She adapted what she had learned from Phineas Parkhurst Quimby, a magnetic healer from Maine, without giving him any credit for it.

Whatever the final verdict on this remarkable woman, nobody can deny her very great talents and the long stretches of ill health she endured, whether or not she had a tendency toward hypochondria. She suffered from frequent bouts of physical and nervous disorders. Her first husband died early. The second one, a dentist, deserted her. She was separated by force from her only child. Poverty was far from unknown to her in her earlier years.

Only her third marriage seemed to have been a happy one. The bride was fifty-three years old at the time of her wedding to Asa Gilbert Eddy, who was a student of hers. He declared that she had cured him from an illness.

Many circumstances pointed Mary Baker Eddy in the direction of spiritual pioneering. An intense religious revival swept her native New England and the East Coast at the time. She liked to read and, being gifted with an excellent mind, she absorbed the contents of difficult books on Western and Eastern philosophy. The Bible remained, of course, the first and foremost item on her reading list.

In a way, the long periods of illness and misfortune were key elements in her mental development. They induced her to look inward and to do a lot of meditating. Thoughts about health were never far from her mind. She became acquainted with several "magnetic" healers of the time. Eventually, she took to comforting other sick people. "I found that I had the power of not only feeling their aches and pains, but the state of their minds." She gained a small reputation of her own as suffering neighbors began to find their way to her door.

But Mrs. Eddy had more in mind than becoming just another local healer. She started formulating a whole system of beliefs in her mind. Whether completely original or not, she was successful in expressing these beliefs in a compact, organized form, and she proved to be a competent and compelling writer. Her foremost literary work is the book, *Science and Health With Key to the Scriptures*. In its form, it is a running commentary on the Old and New Testaments. Its contents form the basis for Christian Science teachings. At every service of the new faith, a passage from the Bible is recited aloud by a lay reader, followed by the corresponding section of *Science and Health* read by a second lay reader.

Like all leading personalities in the history of religion, Mrs. Eddy must have had charisma, the gift of attracting people and awing them with a magnetic personality. Her organizational talent also becomes obvious in the early stages of the movement. That she was allowed to make use of it is the more remarkable when we realize that she lived at a time when males were even more reluctant than today to accept the leadership of a woman.

While many other movements have evaporated quickly with the departure of the leader, Christian Science continues to be in vigorous health. The "mother church" in Boston is a magnificent complex, a showpiece of the city, comprising a vast domed sanctuary, a large publishing plant, and many halls and offices from which the worldwide effort is directed. The number of members is unknown as the church makes it a point not to give out figures.

Among all the unique features of Christian Science, the most striking is the church position on sickness and health. It is radically different from the stand of practically all other religions. Although the leaders maintain that there is much more to Christian Science than the attitude toward illness, this is the real trademark of the religion.

For Mary Baker Eddy, her teachings on health were a direct outgrowth of her basic thoughts on God and man. Primarily, she emphasized the following points, all derived from her study of the Bible:

1. God is spiritual, not material.
2. God is all good.
3. God is eternal.
4. God is perfect.
5. Man is created in the image of God.

From this set of assumptions she went on to reason that since God is all good and perfect, and since man is created in God's image, it follows that man is all good and perfect. A perfect and good God cannot create an imperfect world. Creating what is bad and painful would conflict with God's goodness. It would make Him imperfect.

Therefore, there is no such thing as evil, sickness, or death. They could never come from God. They are not real. What does not exist cannot hurt anybody. People only imagine that they are sick or in pain. If they feel this way they are in error; they do not understand the true nature of God and man. If they did, they would be in perfect control of their bodies, since the physical self is only an image, a reflection of the spiritual self. We are, like God, spiritual beings.

For the devout Christian Scientist, any physical or mental discomfort is only an illusion. The way to get rid of the disturbing illusion is to pray, to study the Bible, and particularly to read *Science and Health* intensively. If this is done, all symptoms will quickly disappear like the warts on the letterwriter's hands.

Even if the Christian Scientist does not succeed on his own in overcoming the feeling of being sick, he does not consult a physician nor does he visit a hospital. Instead, he looks up a Christian Science practitioner. The practitioners have offices and hold office hours just like doctors. They are licensed by the church, but have not undergone any medical training. Instead, they counsel the client in the teachings of Christian Science. They pray with him, interpret Mrs. Eddy's writings to him, and try to put him into a frame of mind in which he will accept the idea that his trouble is not real.

Even those opposed to the Christian Science way will have to admit that an effective practitioner can be of great help to persons who seek him out. To some extent, what he does is a form of psychotherapy.

Mary Baker Eddy, despite all of her ailments, lived to be eighty-nine years old and then died of a heart disease in 1910. Her detractors whispered that she had secretly called in doctors and had taken pills and medicines contrary to her own teachings.

True or not, it hardly detracts from the originality of her message. Nor was it less of a startling revelation to her disciples when they learned that similar thoughts were involved in the sayings of Hindu and Buddhist sages and also in the writings of British and German philosophers. It still took Mrs. Eddy's talent to wrap all this up into a simple package of statements and directives applicable to everyday life in our time.

If a believer sticks to all the tenets of the church, he or she will not take medicines in any form and will not receive shots. The children will not be inoculated against infectious diseases unless it is done at school and the law forbids the parents to interfere.

However, there are nursing homes which are accredited by the church. Invalid members are cared for by Christian Science nurses. The member lets his own conscience decide whether or not to call a doctor or midwife to assist with childbirth. When an accident causes broken bones, it is not unheard of to have a surgeon set them. The church does not penalize a member for seeking such help. It merely points to the many testimonials in the *Christian Science Sentinel* that report complicated bone fractures that just disappeared overnight without any medical assistance after proper prayer and meditation.

As with so many forms of nonmedical healing, there is no doubt that patients suffering from nonorganic illnesses or from purely emotional problems can be helped by following the path of Christian Science. As for the deterioration of tissues and organs and the damage caused by accidents, the answer depends on the faith of the patient. It is a clear positive answer without any "ifs" or "buts" that issues from the mouths of Christian Scientists whose beliefs are firmly rooted in the teachings of Mary Baker Eddy.

Christian Science, now nearly one hundred years old, is the most successful and enduring healing religion. But it is not the only one which sprang from the spiritual unrest of nineteenth-century America. John Alexander Dowie preached that all illness is the work of the devil. Therefore, it can only be combated by prayer and the time-honored laying on of hands. For a while, the headquarters of his followers was in Zion City, a suburb of Chicago. This movement did not last long.

Joseph Smith, the founder of the Church of Jesus Christ of Latter-Day Saints, commonly called the Mormon religion, was credited with healing some of his early followers. However, healing outside the professional medical channels did not remain part of Mormon activities.

Christian Science practitioners are adamant in their assertion, "We are not faith healers." The faith healers admit that illness is real, Christian Science does not. Similar thoughts about the unreality of the body and therefore of anything that is wrong with the body are characteristic of religions that originated in India. They are older than Christian Science. In fact, they existed many hundreds of years before the rise of Christianity itself.

During the Second World War, a great many American soldiers were stationed around the Far East. Communication between America and Eastern Asia was lively. We learned much about the way of life in those countries and also about the religions of Hinduism and Buddhism.

During the last few decades, many Americans and Europeans, especially those of the younger generation, have been strongly attracted by Eastern ideas. They are seeking an alternative to the unsatisfying, materialistic life-style that prevails in the modern city.

On college campuses, in community centers, and over television stations, one can now learn about *yoga*, a view of world and man derived from the thoughts of ancient Hindu sages. There are many branches of yoga, but they all have certain basic elements in common.

A *yogi*, one who practices yoga seriously, feels, not unlike Christian Scientists, that the whole material world is an illusion. The only reality is the universal spirit, a nonpersonal concept of God. The spirit is not somewhere out there beyond the clouds; it is everywhere, all-pervading, both in the universe and inside us. The world spirit or world soul is like an endless ocean, and the souls of all creatures are like rain-drops, which, after a while, fall back into the sea where they dissolve and become part of the world soul.

A yogi is often pictured in the "lotus position." He sits cross-legged with the sole of one foot pressed against the opposite thigh, looking vacantly down at his navel. Yogis assume many positions arrived at by doing body exercises in slow motion. While Westerners may think of these move-ments mainly as physical training, the real yogi performs them only to put himself into the right frame of mind for meditation.

Meditation is the key to the mystic experiences toward which all Eastern thought systems seem to gravitate. It is the quiet withdrawal from all noise and commotion of the world around us. In meditation a person retreats into himself. He makes it possible for the spiritual forces within himself to be released.

While many of us see the goal of our lives in terms of suc-cess and the acquisition of good housing, clothing, and luxury items, Hindu thought presents to man the goal of release from all such ambitions, from the attachment to things and to other people, from all needs and cravings. The only striving should be toward reaching perfection, not in the sense of being per-fectly strong or perfectly powerful, but in the sense of losing one's individuality by spiritual unification with the world soul. The material world around us is a prison. Only by liberating ourselves from it, can we become its masters rather than its slaves. Our own bodies are part of the material world.

[Selvarajan Yesudian, an Indian yogi, tells that as a young boy living in the city of Madras, he was always weak and sickly. He suffered from continuous colds and from frequent bouts with pneumonia. Almost without interruption, he went from illness to illness. All this left him thin and pale with eyes sunken and chest narrow. His father, a famous physician, was unable to help him. He himself felt like an outcast among his schoolmates, since he was excluded from all their games.

In his anguish, he tried physical exercises on his own, but that only made things worse. Finally, he wandered off into the woods by the city. He sought out a practicing yogi he had heard about. The yogi became the boy's *guru*, or teacher.

The guru taught him yoga philosophy and the body postures that went with it. At first, they were very difficult to execute. Several times the new disciple nearly dislocated his legs. He was taught to breathe deeply and slowly and to hold his breath until his lungs almost burst. In time he was able to stand on his head with ease and even to drape a leg over his shoulder without visible effort or sweat.

Within two months his old acquaintances could hardly recognize him. He walked straight, his shoulders had become broader, and his chest had expanded. He suffered no more colds, no more fevers. The boy grew up to be a yogi himself. He set himself the task of bringing the Hindu way to the West, and so he became the guru of many disciples in England and neighboring countries.

He also took up the pen and wrote one of the many popular books on the subject which can be found in almost any bookstore or library. He relates:

Man is spirit clothed in flesh. . . . The purpose of yoga is to make our human consciousness dependent on our will. . . . The final goal is divine consciousness developed to perfection. . . . As we constantly grope in darkness, we pay for our ignorance, and the unequal distribution of forces allows thousands of different diseases to come upon us. . . . Inasmuch as we ourselves have caused our sickness, we must heal our abused bodies ourselves.

The language is difficult, and the thoughts which it tries to express are unfamiliar to us. In trying to understand them, we can summarize that we create our own illnesses because we have imperfect minds, because our animal instincts, our body needs, are in control instead of being controlled by our minds. Fear, worry, and greed are such lower forces. Only when they are overcome can permanent health result. A mind that is in the driver's seat also prevents aging before its time.

According to yoga teachings, even infectious diseases, such as measles or smallpox, have mental causes. Every accident, whether it happens in the kitchen or in the car, is really a form of self-punishment. The yogi feels that the medical techniques taught at universities are insufficient. They treat the disease, but they do not heal the patient. Healing can only come from the patient himself when he succeeds in subordinating his body to the spiritual forces within him.

Many different forms of yoga were developed in India. They all agree on the final goal of human perfection which brings union of individual and world soul, but they propose different ways to reach the goal. The disciple can select the way that best fits his personal needs and background.

Some yoga systems are for the advanced practitioner only. Such persons have already abandoned the material world and live as "holy men" without possessions. We find many such barefoot, homeless men wandering about the countryside of India. They are greatly admired as models of human behavior.

The advanced yogi is supposed to have attained such a high degree of spirituality that his body has become completely unimportant to him. He does not care and does not feel what happens to it. This explains the many stories about holy men who can lie on beds of sharp spikes or walk barefoot on red-hot coals without feeling any pain or even discomfort. Yogis are said to be able to slow down their pulse and breathing, lower their blood pressure, and reduce the other functions of their bodies to the point that it seems as if the physical part of them is only partially alive.

In the Indian town of Bangalore, a yogi was buried in a pit during the course of a scientific experiment. A mound of soil was heaped on top of his body in the sight of several witnesses. A number of instruments had been attached to the yogi's body before the burial. The dials showed a slowdown of heartbeat and other bodily functions to such a degree that the needles hardly indicated any life. It was as if the yogi had simply turned off his whole body apparatus. But after ten hours, he climbed out of the pit, just as alive as he had been before the experiment.

Such ordeals are not for everybody, not even for every adherent of yoga. For the beginner and for the American and European who have been spoiled by more comfortable living patterns, less demanding forms of yoga are recommended. One of them is *Hatha Yoga*, which stresses, beside the body postures and breathing exercises, simple natural food and a generally slow and relaxed approach to all problems that arise. It teaches not so much withdrawal from the company of other humans as making the best use of the life force within us while continuing to function as members of society.

Many Americans have become familiar with the term Transcendental Meditation, TM for short. Courses and pamphlets on TM are being sold to the public through well-organized promotional campaigns which use television, newspaper and magazine ads, and free introductory lectures. Its guru is the Indian yogi, Maharishi Mahesh, but its local teachers are well-groomed Caucasian men and women. TM demands that its adherents set aside twenty minutes each morning and each evening for quiet meditation. When followed according to instructions, this will bring the meditator not only better mental and physical health, but generally a greater ability to face the problems of life, whether at school, in business, or in personal relations with other people.

[Another great religion of the East, Buddhism, is an offshoot of Hinduism. Its founder, Buddha, who walked the earth about five centuries before Jesus, lived and taught against the background of the much older Hindu world. Buddhism spread over many countries, mainly in East Asia, and in the process divided into countless sects. It too has aroused the interest of smaller groups in Europe and America in recent decades. Those sects which have stayed close to the ideas of the founder also speak of perfection as man's spiritual goal. Like the Hindu sages, Buddha stressed the importance of quiet meditation, of looking inward, of the vanity of all material pursuits. Otherwise, he taught, life would be just an endless string of suffering. But by renouncing all ties the soul can reach *Nirvana*, the timeless state of enduring bliss.

Buddha was not directly concerned with maintaining good health; it was of no importance in his framework of ideas. Rather, it followed that a disciple of Buddha had no time to worry about health, and the absence of worry probably makes Buddhists healthier. Buddhist monks live in their own communities under very strict rules which require simple food eaten only once a day, lots of walking in the open air, and, once again, many hours of quiet meditation.

Quite a few thoughtful Americans were immensely impressed by one particular Buddhist sect which arrived here by way of India-China-Japan. This sect is called *Zen*. The Zen devotees lead a communal life under a Zen master, or Roshi. While they also partake of simple food and drink, they surround themselves with natural and manmade beauty. Japanese Zen temples are famous for their exquisite gardens and artistic structures and outdoor sculptures that blend into the natural surroundings. The Zen followers practice graceful ceremonies, such as the often described tea ceremony, but they also engage in rigorous exercises. They practice fencing and dedicate themselves to the art of weaponless self-defense. But all this activity takes second place to the many hours of the day reserved for quiet meditation.

The call for meditation as an antidote to the frantic pace and the frustration of our present society has come from many quarters and taken many forms. All of them believe that the health of body and mind can be maintained and, if need be, regained, by replacing tension with calmness, insecurity with inner peace.

~~~~~~

CHAPTER FIFTEEN

Psychic Healers

JANE WAS THIRTEEN MONTHS OLD and she was as miserable as a baby could be. First, it had been a bad cold that plagued her, and now her ears were infected. She was obviously in terrible pain. Her parents were profoundly distressed listening to her pitiful crying and watching her rubbing her little ears to shreds. The doctor first punctured the eardrum and then prescribed a medicine that made the baby cry in even more anguish.

Grandmother showed up to see if she could help. It was she who decided on her own that it was time to contact Edgar Cayce, the widely known psychic healer. She sent a message to his home in Kentucky asking him to do a "reading" on poor Jane. Cayce responded by following his usual procedure. Jane and her family were completely unknown to him and lived many miles away. Without leaving his home, he willed himself into a deep trance. He could accomplish this within minutes. Otherwise, he could never have coped with the innumerable requests that came from so many different places.

Within an hour, his secretary phoned Jane's parents with the results of the "reading." It gave a detailed diagnosis of the patient whom he had never seen. It then prescribed massages with camphorated oil, mutton tallow, and turpentine, and a medicine to be taken every three or four hours. The drops were completely different from those prescribed earlier by the doctor. By long distance, Edgar Cayce also recommended ample natural fruit juice without sugar.

Jane was treated according to the "reading." On the next day, she was much improved. The family doctor was flabbergasted when he saw the drastic change; he had not been told about the consultation with Edgar Cayce. The remote control treatment continued. It took only one more reading by Mr. Cayce and Jane was on the way to complete recovery.

Edgar LeShan, another psychic healer who is also a trained psychologist, was riding in a car with his wife and some friends. At a sudden stop, the safety belt above the window came loose, and the metal buckle hit Mrs. LeShan in the eye. The pain was excruciating. "Edgar, give me a healing," she cried to her husband. He put his hands around her face and closed his eyes. This is what followed, according to his wife's report:

I felt a tingling sensation combined with a soothing deep heat. My face began to swell and become discolored. Everyone agreed that while I was lucky to have my eye intact, I'd undoubtedly have a monumental shiner. Yet within two hours, the pain, the discoloration, and the swelling had completely disappeared. The psychic healing was a success.

Sally Hammond, a New York newspaperwoman, was told by her doctor that she had a tumor of the breast. He urged an immediate operation, but expressed fears that it might already be too late. Deeply frightened, Sally remembered that she had heard some time ago of a psychic healer who lived in England. She had never set much stock in such matters, but now she was desperate and willing to try anything.

She phoned Mary Rogers and poured out her story over

the intercontinental phone. The woman healer listened patiently. Then, though they had never met, she accurately described Sally's face and hairdo and also the dress she was wearing at the moment. This was to assure the American woman of her ability to help. Then she arranged for a course of action.

> Just link up with me once a day at 10 P.M. our time. Find a quiet place and concentrate on reaching me. I will be with you despite the three-thousand-mile distance. Shut everything else from your mind, and you will reach me. We will keep it up for a week.

When the week was over, Sally had lost her fear. Her mind was filled with the strong conviction that she was out of danger. Without further hesitation, she underwent the operation. A growth was removed from her breast. She was not at all surprised when she was told that it had been found harmless. Sally ascribed the result to Mary Rogers' power. From then on she became an ardent student of psychic healing and related supernatural events.

Here were three cases of healing. Each was handled in a different way, yet all three are examples of a trend that surprises the student of human history. We seem to be returning to the ideas held by our ancestors in the very remote past, but the ideas are now expressed in the language and symbolism of the twentieth century. In this age of the most marvelous accomplishments of science and technology, the age of computers and moon landings, thousands of people are again talking of spirits and ghosts, of magic forces, of events which defy the laws of gravity, and of spooky acts performed by persons with mysterious powers.

What was earlier in our century considered pure childish superstition is now seriously discussed by both educated and uneducated people. Words such as *clairvoyance, telepathy,* and *telekinesis* slip into the spoken and written language. Clairvoyance is the ability to see and know what is hidden. The clairvoyant asserts that he can distinguish what is happening in faraway places and also what is going to happen in the future. Telepathy transmits and receives messages from any distance by purely spiritual means; this happens instantly as if through the use of radio or radar. By telekinesis, the person gifted with special psychic powers can make things move without touching them or using any kind of physical force.

A *medium* is a person who claims to possess unexplainable powers that go beyond the known strength of the body and the proven capacity of the mind. We find mediums who say they can find missing persons who are unknown to them. Others know instantly when an accident happens hundreds of miles away, and still others try to demonstrate that they can bend iron nails without using their hands or instruments.

The fortune-teller is a well-known folk figure, and the crystal ball part of her inevitable paraphernalia. It has even become a figure of speech. Sybil Leek, a medium who engages in various forms of psychic activity, explains that the famed crystal ball serves as a point of concentration similar to the strong light often used by the hypnotist.

All these strange abilities come into play when we speak of psychic healing. Some healers refer to themselves as modern witches.

Ironically, England, which two centuries ago spearheaded the industrial revolution, is now a particularly fertile area for psychic and spiritualistic activities. Several thousand psychic healers go about their business in the island kingdom, apparently without encountering much harassment from government or the medical profession.

Psychic healers borrow freely from older beliefs and philosophies. Some, like Sybil Leek, claim to practice pre-Christian witchcraft. Others speak of reincarnation. Many engage in and recommend various forms of meditation, and quite a few resemble faith healers in their words and gestures. But there exists an essential difference. Faith healing requires a belief in God and in God's power to heal through man. The ailing person must seek out the faith healer actively, while a psychic healer will treat a person who is not even aware of his existence and who may believe in some exotic religion or in none at all. Belief has nothing to do with the success of the healing—at least that is what the psychic healer maintains.

Edgar LeShan tells that a friend asked him to heal his wife who was three thousand miles away. She had such severe pain in her right arm that for six weeks she could not do any work which required the use of her hands. The next day Mr. LeShan called the friend, who had forgotten about the request and had said nothing to his wife. When the healer inquired about her health, the answer was, "Oh, my God, I had forgotten all about it. She is flipping pancakes."

Some healers modestly disclaim any personal magic powers. Their explanation for their strange cures is that the spirits of dead people contact them and give them the knowledge and the skills to be successful. Spiritualists strongly believe that the dead are still around and can be contacted if one knows the right method. In their *séances*, spiritualists try to make such contacts. Sometimes the medium claims to hear the voice of the deceased speak. Or the departed makes himself understood by strange knocks and other noises. While the living are limited in knowledge, after death the curtains are lifted from many secrets, and the hidden becomes known. Therefore, the spirits of the departed can furnish advice and help that would not otherwise be available to us.

Healer Estelle Roberts asserts that she always acts upon

the advice of a dead Indian medicine man whom she calls
Red Cloud. He is her "spirit guide":

> Red Cloud has a band of spirit helpers which includes some
> who were doctors on earth. . . . Red Cloud, the great spirit
> physician, is continuing his work for our heavenly Father here
> on this earth, curing and helping both soul and body.

Estelle Roberts recounts incident after incident in which
she called on the invisible Red Cloud for guidance when
confronted with a sick person. The ghostly Indian always
came through with just the right answer. Estelle did what
he told her and the patient rose, miraculously cured of whatever had been bothering him.

In the spiritualist view, the spirits of dead relatives and
friends retain the same loving concern for the living that they
had shown before their demise. Long deceased medical pioneers are still around, unseen, helping the sick by way of
giving instructions to a living medium. One healer reports
that he has frequently held consultations with Lister and
Pasteur, the great pioneers of modern medical science.

Strange goings-on were reported from a small mountain
town in southern Brazil. There José Arigo, a kindly, simple
family man, was leading a very unusual double existence.
Day after day he went to his lowly routine job as a minor
civil servant. After spending the required number of unex-
citing working hours there, he returned home to find as many
as two hundred people waiting for him. They were afflicted
with every conceivable kind of disease.

Arigo went inside an old dilapidated church close to his
house which had become a sort of clinic. He disappeared into
a little cubicle, and when he emerged again after a short while
he had become a different person. His voice now sounded

deep and guttural, whereas it had been soft and high before. He spoke with a heavy German accent although he had never known a foreign language. His whole manner of behavior had drastically changed. He was now acting like the commanding officer of a Prussian regiment of soldiers.

An old blind man stepped forward. Arigo examined him quickly, then grabbed a used paring knife from the table, and without hesitation, plunged it into the man's eye. The watchers recoiled in horror, but the patient did not even flinch. There was no pain, no blood. Within a minute, Arigo had removed a cataract and sent the old man on his way after writing out a prescription. The prescription had been scribbled at high speed. The handwriting bore no resemblance to Arigo's ordinary lettering, and the contents showed a degree of medical and pharmaceutical knowledge way above the level of even the most educated townsman.

As far as Arigo was concerned, the case was closed. He wiped the knife clean on his shirt and was ready for the next patient. The operations for tumors and cysts continued at a rapid pace until late into the night.

The performance baffled medical and legal investigators, who turned up in droves. All that they could figure out was that they were dealing with a case of split personality. This is a well-known severe mental disease. But Arigo had no other symptoms of being mentally disturbed. Whatever it was that ailed him, however, it was a blessing to hundreds of people.

It turned out that when Arigo faced his patients, he ceased to be the simple Brazilian civil servant and became Dr. Adolph Fritz, a brilliant German surgeon. Dr. Fritz died in the First World War, one year after Arigo was born. The spirit of the dead physician had chosen the Brazilian as the medium to carry on his prematurely interrupted work. At least that was the explanation preferred by Arigo's numerous supporters.

Edgar Cayce, the psychic healer from Kentucky, also harbored two distinct personalities in his body, although he operated out of entirely different surroundings. On one level he was a competent professional photographer, a friendly Sunday school teacher, and a good husband and father. But at will he could put himself into a trance that resembled a deep hypnotic sleep. In that state, he instantly recognized the nature of illnesses whether contracted by persons present or absent, known or unknown to him. He then prescribed effective treatments which were, in many instances, unknown to physicians. To treat an absent patient, all he needed was the name and address. When he returned to his normal waking state, he had no recollection of what had occurred during the trance. His medical advice could only be followed up because people who were with him during the trance wrote down or repeated afterward what he had said. When Edgar Cayce was not in a trance, he knew no more about medical matters than any other layman.

How do psychic healers try to explain their obscure powers? A British woman psychic tells that she asks the patient to concentrate not on his illness, but on the healer. The healer, in turn, pictures the patient in her mind as healthy and vigorous. This sounds good, but it still does not account for the influence of the picture in the healer's mind on the reality of the patient's body, especially when the suffering person is far away.

Healers use mystic language which is hard for the non-psychic to follow. They claim to possess a more than ordinary amount of life energy.

The healer has an abundant supply of life energy, the patient too little. This is the reason for his sickness. The task is then to pass on some quantity of the healer's energy into the life system of the client. Perhaps we can picture this process in our minds by thinking of a weak car battery that is being recharged by connecting it with a strong battery.

From the healer, the current flows into the patient even though no cables connect the two.

Spiritual healers often report that after a healing session they feel completely drained. In attempting to dominate the patient's physical and mental system, they exhaust their own energy. They cannot go on treating patient after patient as a doctor may do during a day in his office. They must get lots of rest in between cases to restore their inner resources.

This life energy dwells not only within the body of the spiritualist, but surrounds it like the halo surrounds the head of a saint in religious pictures. But this halo, known as the *aura* or *corona*, is not confined to the top of the head; it is an extension of the personal life force radiating from the whole surface of the body.

Although this corona is invisible to all who are not trained in spiritualism, methods have been developed to photograph it. It is a twist of irony that reports of such photographs first came from the Soviet Union, even though Marxist philosophy —which is the official way of thinking there—denies the existence of anything that is not material.

This so-called Kirlian photograph is said to illustrate that streams of light flow from the healer's hand into the patient during the healing session. After the healing is complete, the corona of the healer has become dimmer and that of the patient brighter and more radiant.

Many psychic healers consider their work a regular occupation. They charge for services or depend on voluntary donations. The rapport they can attain with the public establishes their success. Because of this, psychic healing attracts all sorts of frauds who exploit the gullibility of others. When people need a healer, they are usually depressed, and their defenses are down and their judgment impaired.

Then there are those members of the psychic guild who regard their gift with humility, and they want others to receive the benefit of it. They do not think in terms of financial gain. In one American city, a group of spiritualists meets every Wednesday night for "healing meditations." People who are sick or troubled are invited to call a downtown office and leave their names. They are then asked to retire to a quiet place on that Wednesday evening and "keep time" mentally with the healing group. When the group has assembled, one member reads off the names of all who have called in. Then they try to direct their collective healing power to those unseen and mostly unknown patients. They sit in complete silence in a close circle with arms linked. In this way, they hope to raise "healing vibrations," which will strengthen the patient's own will to get well.

As is to be expected with any large group of people, psychic healers have different temperaments and attitudes. There are those who surround their healing procedures with deep secrecy, while others maintain that everybody can learn the craft provided they are themselves physically and emotionally healthy and have a strong desire to help ill people. Psychic healers propose that most of us have more life energy than we ordinarily use.

Probably just as old as the belief in the existence of spirits is the belief that human fate is connected with the movements of the stars in the sky. *Astrology* was practiced by the ancient Babylonians and Assyrians thousands of years ago. Christian kings and emperors had their court astrologers, and in southern Asia weddings and other important events are still scheduled only after consultation with the local astrologer.

Like spiritism, astrology declined with the rise of the natural sciences. It was relegated to the confines of old wives' tales and children's stories. But in the last several years, astrology has experienced a resurgence. Particularly among the young people of our own society, it has become a wide-spread cult of sorts.

The term astrology is often confused with the similar sounding word astronomy. Astronomy is an acknowledged field of natural science and research. It explores outer space and all the bodies which move in it: moons, planets, fixed stars, meteors, and so forth. With the help of telescopes mounted in domed observatories and through complicated mathematical computations, astronomers devise theories about the origin and life span of the natural universe. To this end, they borrow findings from other sciences, such as geology, chemistry, and biology.

By contrast—and the contrast is very evident—astrology rests on an assumption that escapes any proof by scientific methods. It asserts that the movements of the stars have a dominant influence on man's fate. Actually, the early astrol-oger-priests were also astronomers. They studied the nature of the stars as best they could with the naked eye, but they did it primarily in order to predict from their findings what would happen to men on earth.

Today astrology is big business. Articles and broadcasts on the subject draw large audiences. Astrological terms creep into casual conversation. One can hear them in popular songs and see them emblazoned on T-shirts and other clothing.

When astrologers make predictions from the stars, their interest is centered on the Zodiac, the portion of the sky through which sun, moon, and stars move from east to west. They speak of the twelve Signs of the Zodiac, which are twelve recurring combinations of the sun and other stars. Into each combination the astrologer reads a number of special meanings. In astrological terms we are now moving into the Age of Aquarius, one of the Signs of the Zodiac.

In order to predict a person's future, the astrologer draws up a *horoscope*. He or she diagrams the position of moon, planets, and stars at important moments of that person's life, especially the exact time of his birth. From the horoscope, conclusions are drawn about the subject's character and in-clinations, his tendency to run into certain difficulties, and his chances of success.

For the believer in astrology, the horoscope provides valu-able advice on what decisions he should make about his life. This includes decisions about his health. The horoscope will warn him that he has a tendency to contract certain illnesses and would do well to take precautions. By a correct reading of the stars one can avoid accidents or pick the best time to undergo a major operation. Astrologers even diagnose ill-nesses, not through a medical examination, but by observing the position of the planets, since each planet represents an organ of the human body.

According to a report found in an astrological publication, five hundred people afflicted with cancer were found to have certain features in their horoscopes in common. Had they realized the situation early enough, they could have received treatment before the illness had progressed to the point of extreme danger.

When an astrologer meets a friend who suffers from a severe mental depression, he will advise him not to consult a psychiatrist, but to study his own astrological birth chart, particularly the relative positions of the moon and planets in it. This will give him the best clue for effective counter-measures.

The idea that all this majestic movement in the heavens must have some meaning for our life span and our health seems unshakeable to a good many human beings.

CHAPTER SIXTEEN

Shaman and Doctor

THE SHAMAN is still with us.

From the distant beginnings of life until the present day, he has attended to people in pain and in fear, the wounded, the aged, the dying. His names have been many: medicine man, witch doctor, king, priest, magnetizer, Christian Scientist, yogi, psychic healer. Each name represents a set of values, a world view.

Among the healers who practiced their art during the past centuries were many who sincerely believed in their special powers and in their mission to remove misery. There were others too, however—the quacks, who knew they were fooling their clients.

Success did not always accompany the efforts of the healer even when he understood his capabilities. That the quack failed most of the time was no surprise to anyone, least of all to him. We do not hear much about failures. It is the successes that are advertised by word of mouth and in print and that are praised in ecstatic testimonials. A physician who writes very critically about miracle cures remarks:

> If you would know the value of an elixir, ask the one for whom it did not work. If you would know the power of a healer, ask

the patient whom he cannot cure. Even when the sick felt relief after the healer had done his work, it was, more often than not, temporary.

A psychologist was quoted as saying:

> You can psyche a person up to the point where he is convinced he has no pain. You can stop a tuberculosis patient from coughing, but he can still die of tuberculosis.

This temporary feeling of relief can be extremely dangerous when it delays competent medical help until it is too late.

Still, at all times, in all places, the most unlikely sorts of healers—quacks included—could point to impressive numbers of successes. Their triumphant stories could fill entire libraries.

How can we explain the beneficial results of practitioners whom all the modern experts would judge unqualified? Here are some facts to consider.

First of all, many wounds, aches, and illnesses cure themselves in time without the benefit of any outside help. Our body is very resilient. Its organs generally operate way below capacity like an engine that runs consistently in low gear. But when this engine is revved up to full speed, it can do marvelous things. Oftentimes the patient recovers by making use of his own resources, but the healer gets the credit.

Even people suffering from very serious chronic illnesses, such as multiple sclerosis, may suddenly experience a startling improvement which the physicians call a *regression*. This gives the patient an enormous boost in morale, but later comes the tragic letdown when the improvement turns out to be only temporary.

We should also remember that a good many weaknesses of the body are caused by defects in our minds. Doctors estimate that anywhere from 50 to 80 percent of the people knocking at the doors of their offices suffer from psychosomatic diseases. Their discomforts are real. Nobody can deny that these people are actually plagued by ulcers, acne, nervous tics, or migraine headaches. But neither physical examination nor chemical tests can ascertain any reason why the body should produce such disorders. Nothing permanent can be accomplished by medication or diets or surgery. The physical illness is triggered by obstacles to emotional well-being. Such obstacles must disappear before any cure can be permanent.

Never underestimate the power of faith. Faith can arouse body and mind to accomplishments that astound. It may be faith in the universal God or in a special god; in miracle-working places, statues, or relics; even in stones and various assortments of charms.

In order to recover from sickness we must have the will to get well. The will is the key factor, and it is not always present. We know that, under great stress, people have willed themselves to die—and they died. Persons under voodoo death spells gave up the will to live and so made the spell come true. Inmates of Nazi concentration camps, faced with the horror and hopelessness of their situation, gave up and died; others, under the same conditions, preserved the will to live and survived.

A shrewd, experienced healer knows how to arouse and fortify the will to life and health. His most potent tool is the power of suggestion. If he handles it well, he can inspire hope and confidence. The successful healer possesses charisma. He communicates optimism. Instead of bewailing his misery, the patient is led to picture himself as potentially strong and vibrant. As one psychic healer put it, "I help the patient use his own self-repairing abilities more fully."

The patient may become so strongly impressed by the healer's charisma that he feels he must get well, if for no other reason than to not let the healer down. He has to show himself worthy of the great man's trust.

Mass suggestion can be more powerful than the communication between two single persons. Some of the famous faith healers know this well. They prepare their gatherings carefully to achieve maximum effect.

Once aroused, the will to recover is strengthened by the use of rituals and symbols: the wand and feathers of the witch doctor, robes, lights and ornaments, chants, processionals and dances. Perhaps stronger than any other symbolic effect is the body contact between the healer and the afflicted: the touch, the laying on of hands, the massaging. The sick person feels the physical nearness of somebody who tries to help, who is concerned.

Seeking out the healing agent may call for a trip away from home; for example, to a religious shrine or to a healing resort, a spa. Even before the destination is reached, the change of surroundings, the new impressions and new sights can raise the spirits. The traveler is distracted from the eternal broodings about his own troubles. The cure itself is at times preceded or followed by periods of waiting, of rest and relaxation. All this is a good antidote for illness and helps with the recovery, especially when shared with many others who go through the same experiences.

These various elements and many more have kept alive the occupation of lay healing and will probably continue to do so in the foreseeable future. All this in spite of the stupendous progress of scientific medicine in the last two hundred years.

The learned doctor of medicine, possessor of many academic honors and enormous prestige, probably scoffs at the miracle worker and the psychic healer. With some justification, he points to the dangers that can result from the activities of those unlicensed competitors.

The lay healer then gets even with the physician. At the revival service or at the séance, he talks about the futility of the scientific approach and points with glee to those sick persons that the physicians have been unable to help but whom he has been able to heal.

Yet are the two forms of healing really so far apart? With closer observation, we are surprised to find quite a few similarities. It turns out that there is considerable overlapping; there is some common ground.

Lay healers have always handed out medicines, treated wounds, and done what is now called by a fancier name— physical therapy. They possessed considerable knowledge that was passed on to the initiates by word of mouth. Shamans and witches collected roots and herbs that had healing powers. Some of these old remedies have been retained as ingredients in the modern drugs dispensed in our pharmacies.

The taboos which lay healers placed on certain foods kept people out of harm's way. Although they ordered bathing and cleansing only as part of a ritual, the salutory effect on health was obvious. The yogi's admonition to eat sparsely and mainly of natural foods, to keep away from alcohol and drugs, to face the day calmly and unhurriedly, amounted to sound medical and psychiatric advice.

Osteopathic healers recognized the value of body massage. They used to overdo it, but more recently they, and to a lesser extent the chiropractors, are acquiring a sound knowledge of the structure and functions of the whole human body.

While the lay healers anticipated many procedures of modern medicine, the professors in their university clinics began to borrow certain tools from the shaman.

Any doctor who takes his profession seriously knows that his patients are affected not only by what he writes on the prescription pad, but also by what kind of a person he is. The gentle and understanding family doctor, where he still exists, inspires a high degree of confidence. His power of suggestion is not unlike that of the successful faith healer or the old magnetizer. Lots of people believe so strongly in *their* doctor that they feel he can do no wrong. With unlimited trust, they put themselves into his hands.

By touching the patient, by feeling his pulse and listening to his heartbeat, the physician performs the scientific equivalent of the laying on of hands.

The patient is disappointed if he is told to go home and just wait for whatever troubles him to disappear in a natural way. This may be the best and also the least costly advice, yet the visitor wants his doctor to perform some act, some visible ritual on him. If nothing else, he expects to at least take away a prescription.

Physicians are thoroughly aware of the *placebo* effect. A placebo, we may recall, is a harmless but medically useless substance which is prescribed just to keep the patient happy and content and to give him the satisfaction that he received something in return for his money. Chances are that he will not come back the next time he is sick if he cannot carry something away with him. The placebo may be a pill which contains nothing but sugar. Yet in numerous instances the sick person takes the pill and soon after reports how much it has helped him. He expected to get well from taking the worthless substance, and he did. "The placebo effect is one of the most powerful things known to medicine," declares Dr. Elmer Green, a medical researcher.

A paralyzed man who lived in a remote rural area was "cured" when the nurse stuck a thermometer into his mouth to take his temperature. Never having seen this procedure before, he thought it was part of the treatment and, as far as he was concerned, it worked. A woman claimed a similar improvement after she had undergone a chest x-ray as part of her medical checkup.

Pain is a state of mind which may or may not have been brought about by disturbances in the body. Being mental, it can be removed by influences on the mind.

The priest and witch doctor perform in an impressive visual setting, but so do the physician, the psychiatrist, and the hypnotist. They create their own rituals and symbolism which cannot fail to affect deeply an ailing person who is hungry for an unusual, encouraging experience. The expectant air that pervades the waiting room, the closed door to the inner sanctum, the final call into the presence of the person who has the answers—all this has its effect on the patient even before any real treatment is begun.

There are the white-capped nurses, the surgeons in outfits a bit like green space suits, the mysterious dials and blips of the monitors. The whole impressive collection of sounds, sights, and smells of the modern hospital introduces the newcomer into a world completely different from the familiar rhythm of home life. Entering this world with awe and trepidation, the person seeking help is strongly impressed with the feeling that all this high-powered machinery cannot fail to bring him relief.

The good healer is a convincing persuader. What he suggests becomes the client's own will. Hypnosis deals specifically with techniques of strong suggestion. All the lay healers, past and present, have to some extent been hypnotists, even though they may not have been familiar with the term. Hypnosis was once the activity of quacks and entertainers at fairs and vaudeville shows. Now it has been accepted into the area of respected science. It is taught to students at universities and is described and analyzed by scholars in many learned books. The *hypnotherapist* has become an acknowledged member of the healing community.

Suggestion and persuasion are the most basic stock in trade of all psychotherapists, whatever their special approach. Psy-

chotherapy in one form or another is dispensed by hypnothera-
pists, psychoanalysts, psychiatrists with medical degrees, and
psychologists and specialists in various forms of counseling.
Personal rapport and communication are the underlying features in all cases.

The psychic healer explains the effects of the healer-patient
contact in mystic terms which are only comprehensible to
other mystics. The explanations used by the scientist rest on
completely different assumptions.

Who can deny with complete certainty that some individuals may indeed have a gift of healing that cannot be explained
in scientific terms? Life and death, earth and space still contain secrets that remain unrevealed. Most of us will not want
to rely on miracle workers for treatment, but it would be
hard to disprove that some persons seem to possess strange
powers which they can use for the good of others.

We can say with some justification that medical and lay healing have influenced each other in the past. At present they
appear to be moving even closer together. A case in point is
the recent appearance of *biofeedback*, which is receiving lots
of attention in the media. In their experiments, researchers
place electrodes and sensors on the skin of volunteers, mainly
in the region of the skull. Then the volunteers are wired to
monitoring devices that have various lights and dials. It has
been found that the human organism generates a weak amount
of electrical energy. When amplified it will register on the
monitor. The flashing of the lights, sound beeps, and the
movement of the needles on the dials show the subject's blood
pressure, muscle tension, skin temperature, and brain function.
As these functions increase or decrease, the subject gets a
feedback by observing the signals to which he is wired.

Now follows the moment when the medic and the psychic

seem to reach out toward each other. It has long been assumed that certain of our muscle movements are subject to our will while others are strictly involuntary. Walking, playing basketball, drinking coffee, or singing the school anthem result from voluntary muscle action; but willpower has nothing to do, so it was thought, with the heartbeat or movement of blood through the arteries or food through the digestive system.

Now we are being told that we can even influence those functions through our will. We can learn to tap powers which rest within our own minds and watch them go to work on our bodies. The yogis of India have taught similar ideas for a long time.

The researchers hope that biofeedback will help us train our minds so that they can lower our blood pressure and slow down and relax muscle tension. We will be able to measure our own progress by watching the feedback signals. It is the person attached to the end of the wires whose behavior determines how the lights flash and the needles move. As in so many other human activities, practice and training should improve our feedback performance.

All this is still pretty much in the experimental stage. But there are good prospects that, with the help of biofeedback, epileptics will eventually be able to control their dangerous spasms. Other possibilities are the easing of asthma attacks, migraine headaches, sleeplessness, and muscle tics. Inveterate optimists in the field even dream of the control of heart disease by biofeedback.

Headaches are perhaps the most common minor aggravation of life. Yet they are a very difficult obstacle for the medical researcher to tackle. Now spokesmen for biofeedback research give us hope that we will be able to regulate the flow of blood to various parts of the body, including the brain, by sheer willpower. Once we can raise or lower the amount of blood streaming to the brain, we will have licked the bedeviling problem of nagging headaches.

Miss Cass Moreland is a cerebral palsy victim who cannot walk, talk, or use her hands to write. Recently, a special biofeedback machine was constructed for her. With the help of electrodes placed on her forehead, she can now send out signals which are conducted through wires to an amplifier. The strengthened signals activate a specially designed typewriter. The fact that she can express herself in writing (typing) makes it possible for her to attend college in spite of her severe physical handicap.

Biofeedback is the modern version of the age-old attempt to make the mind the master instead of the slave of the body. Once perfected it will train people to be in control of their own life functions. "Biofeedback is the yoga of the West," declared Dr. Green, one of the pioneers in this new field of research.

The circle is closing. First there were the shaman and his successors whose tools were magic, faith, and suggestion. With the growing knowledge of anatomy and physiology, of chemistry and bacteriology, scientific medicine separated itself from the older healing arts. The sciences gave us a new, completely different understanding of ourselves and of our vulnerability. Now the separated systems of healing seem to be moving closer together again, if ever so slightly.

Prospects are excellent that the medical sciences will go on to reach new heights of progress. In our laboratories, new cures will be developed, perhaps even more startling than what was achieved in the last fifty years. Some diseases which still plague us, such as the various forms of cancer, might be eliminated as major threats. The end of the average life span might be pushed back even farther than it has been already.

But people will remain mortal. And with mortality we will retain the fear of death, of aging, of pain and helplessness.

In their frustration as they face those remaining dangers and the new ones which they will create, in their need to find support from the outside and to build up inner strength, people will continue to turn to every conceivable kind of helper. There seems to be room for both the shaman and the surgeon, and also for some combinations of the two.

Suggested Further Readings

Atkinson, Donald T. *Magic, Myth and Medicine*. Cleveland: World, 1956.

Blatty, William P. *The Exorcist*. New York: Harper & Row, 1971.

Blythe, Peter. *Hypnotism: Its Power and Practice*. New York: Taplinger, 1971.

Carter, Mary E., and McGarey, W. E. *Edgar Cayce on Healing*. New York: Paperback Library, 1972.

Coué, Emil. *Self-Mastery through Autosuggestion*. New York: American Library, 1922.

Fischbein, Morris. *The Medical Follies*. New York: Boni & Liveright, 1925.

Flammonde, Paris. *The Mystic Healers*. New York: Stein & Day, 1974.

Fleming, Alice. *Psychiatry: What's It All About?* Chicago: Cowles, 1972.

Goldsmith, Margaret L. *Franz Anton Mesmer: A History of Mesmerism*. Garden City, N.Y.: Doubleday, 1934.

Haggard, Howard W. *The Doctor in History*. New Haven, Conn.: Yale University Press, 1934.

———. *Devils, Drugs and Doctors*. New York: Cardinal, 1929.

Hammond, Sally. *We Are All Healers*. New York: Harper & Row, 1974.

Holbrook, Stuart. *The Golden Age of Quackery*. New York: Macmillan, 1959.

Jacob, Dorothy. *Cures and Curses*. New York: Taplinger, 1967.

Jennings, Gary. *Black Magic, White Magic*. New York: Dial Press, 1964.

Jensen, Ann. *Franz Anton Mesmer*. New York: Garrett, 1967.

Lawrence, Robert M. *Primitive Psychotherapy and Quackery*. New York: Houghton Mifflin, 1910.

Leek, Sybil. *Diary of a Witch*. New York: Signet, 1969.

LeShan, Lawrence. *The Medium, the Mystic and the Physicist*. New York: Viking, 1974.

Major, Ralph. *Faiths That Healed*. New York: Appleton-Century, 1940.

Maple, Eric. *Magic, Medicine and Quackery*. South Brunswick, N.J.: Barnes, 1968.

McKown, Robin. *Pioneers in Mental Health*. New York: Dodd, Mead, 1961.

Métraux, Alfred. *Voodoo in Haiti*. New York: Shocken, 1972.

Meyer, Donald B. *The Positive Thinkers: A Study of the American Quest for Health, Wealth and Personal Power from Mary Baker Eddy to Norman Vincent Peale*. Garden City, N.J.: Doubleday, 1965.

Nolen, William. *Healing: A Doctor in Search of a Miracle*. New York: Random House, 1975.

Podmore, Frank. *From Mesmer to Christian Science: A Short History of Mental Healing*. New Hyde Park, N.Y.: University Books, 1963.

Rose, Louise. *Faith Healing*. New York: Penguin, 1971.

Seifert, Shirley. *The Medicine Man*. Philadelphia, Pa.: Lippincott, 1971.

Sperber, Perry A. *Drugs, Demons, Doctors and Disease*. St. Louis, Mo.: Green, 1973.

Valentini, Tom. *Psychic Surgery*. Chicago: Regnery, 1973.

Worall, A., and Worall, O. *The Gift of Healing*. New York: Harper, 1965.

Yesudian, S., and Haich, E. *Yoga and Health*. 9th ed., London: Unwin, 1966.

Zweig, Stefan. *Mental Healers*. New York: Viking, 1932.

(See also numerous stories in magazines and newspapers, and announcements of public lectures on various topics discussed in the book.)

Index

ABOUT THE AUTHOR

ALFRED APSLER was born in Vienna, Austria, in 1907 and is now an American citizen. He began writing in his student years, and had been a contributor to newspapers and magazines in Europe and the United States and author of trade books and textbooks. For seventeen years he was professor of social science and history at Clark College in Vancouver, Washington, where he lives with his wife and is active in community affairs. He has two grown children.